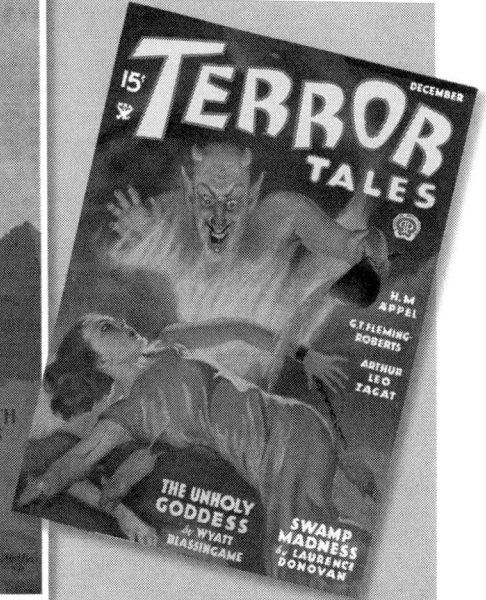

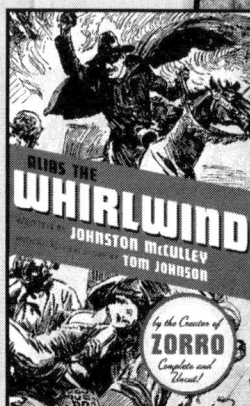

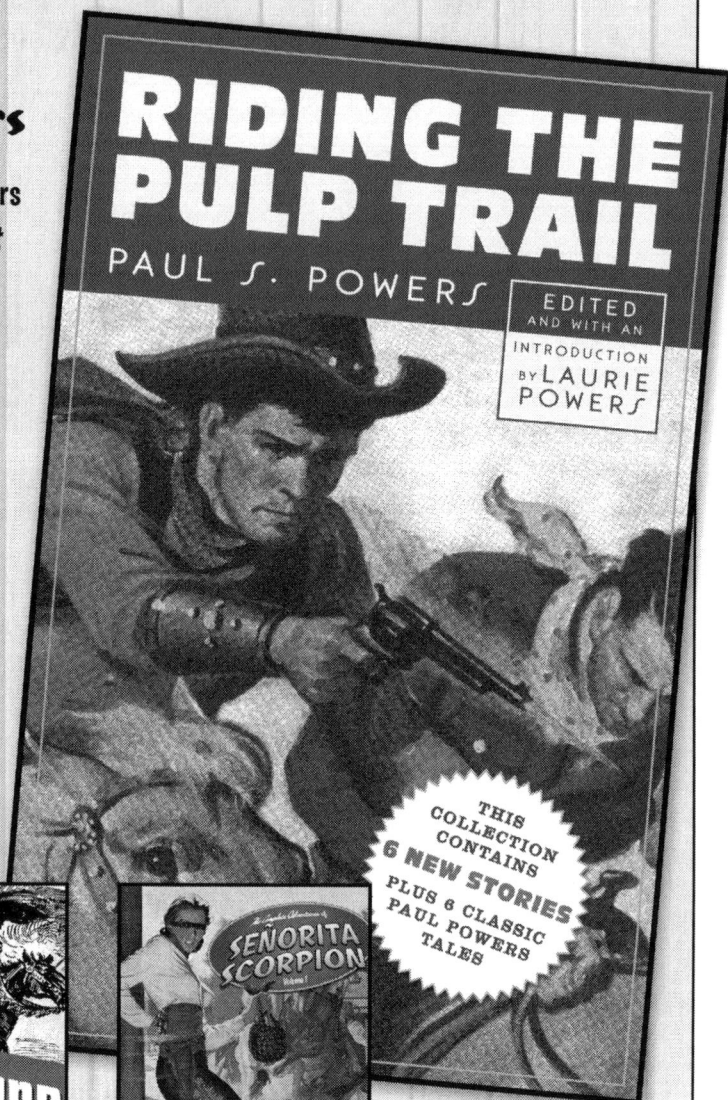

NUMBER 33 ◆ SPRING 2012

BLOOD 'N' THUNDER

ADVENTURE ◆ MYSTERY ◆ MELODRAMA

Ed Hulse
Editor & Publisher

Chris Kalb
Art Director

Mark Trost
Chief Kibitzer

Rick Scheckman
Disgraced Secret Service Agent

Special Thanks to: Martin Grams Jr., Morgan Holmes, Matt Moring, Will Murray.

Blood 'n' Thunder is published four times yearly by Ed Hulse, 2467 Route 10 East, Bldg. 15, Apt. 4B, Morris Plains, NJ 07950. For advertising rates and other information, please e-mail bnteditor@yahoo.com.

Single copy price: $11.95.
One-year (four-issue) subscription: $40.
Please make all checks payable to Ed Hulse. *Blood 'n' Thunder* copies and subscriptions can also be purchased via Paypal; payments should be made out to Ed and sent to bnteditor@yahoo.com.

DEPARTMENTS

FEATURE ARTICLES & REPRINTS

EDITORIAL COMMENTS

Many of you are receiving this issue along with the previous one, and you're probably wondering why. The answer is simple: Since the double issue was so late, I decided to assemble another in a hurry to get back on schedule. Hence, you're actually getting the Spring issue during Spring.

Of course, some compromises had to be made. There's no letter column because, obviously, as this issue was going to press most of you had still not seen 31/32. Hopefully, some of you will be moved to comment on that 234-page extravaganza and next issue's "Epistolary Exchange" will be a humdinger.

I've taken the liberty once again of using some "repurposed" copy, although the articles in question have been significantly altered for their appearance in these pages. My piece on the 1940 Shadow movie serial, written for one of Anthony Tollin's Sanctum Books reprint volumes, was published six months ago. Since then some new facts about the serial have come to light and, in addition to inserting them, I've also clarified and expanded upon points made in the earlier draft. Additionally, I reedited the essay from beginning to end. So the *BnT* version is substantially changed from the one some of you may have read in the Sanctum Press reprint. And it's accompanied by different illustrations.

Likewise, I've retooled Martin Grams Jr.'s excellent history of the short-lived *Green Lama* radio show, a comprehensive survey posted to his blog in several parts some time back. Being an exhaustive researcher, Martin always unearths minutiae other scholars have missed, but in the interest of offering *BnT* readers a smoother-flowing piece, I've streamlined his original work somewhat. Those of you who would like to see the complete version are encouraged to buy the upcoming Altus Press volume of *Green Lama* pulp reprints (advertised in this issue), which will include Martin's survey in its entirety.

ED HULSE

As always, I appreciate his generosity in allowing me to excerpt his books and articles, and I also want to thank Altus head honcho Matt Moring for letting me use the material here.

Making its print debut is Will Murray's article on the Spider's fragile emotional state, a fascinating take on the character that should particularly intrigue those who have not yet read novels from this long-running series. If you belong to that increasingly small group and find your interest piqued by Will's piece, please note that some of our advertisers offer reprinted Spider yarns in a variety of formats. Girasol Collectables, for example, publishes facsimiles of the pulp magazines themselves in addition to two-for-one reprint volumes with new covers and reset type. Age of Aces Press is still selling its deluxe trade-paperback edition of *The Spider vs. the Empire State*, which collects the 1938 "Black Police" trilogy for

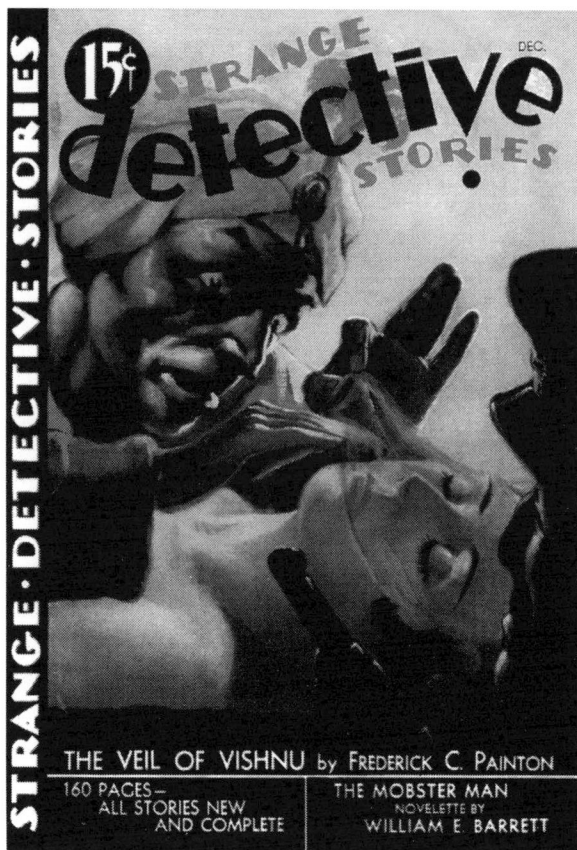

THE VEIL OF VISHNU by FREDERICK C. PAINTON

160 PAGES —
ALL STORIES NEW
AND COMPLETE

THE MOBSTER MAN
NOVELETTE BY
WILLIAM E. BARRETT

the first time between two covers. Will Murray is currently hard at work on a series of Spider audiobooks being sold by Radio Archives; you can find ads for them in the following pages. These adapt the original stories, including a couple mentioned in his article.

Speaking of facsimile reprints, fully one third of this issue is devoted to William E. Barrett's "The Mobster Man," originally published in the December 1933 issue of *Strange Detective Stories*, a short-lived but generally meritorious mystery pulp. I wouldn't normally allot so many pages of a normal-sized *BnT* issue to reprinted fiction, but "Mobster Man" deserves special recognition. Barrett is one of the relatively few pulpsters to achieve major success outside the rough-paper field. He began writing fiction in the late Twenties, selling primarily to Western and avia-

tion pulps for many years. As near as I've been able to determine, "Mobster Man" was his second published detective yarn. Very likely it was the first to feature Dean Culver, "the Blue Barrel."

Barrett had a flair for medium-to-hard-boiled mystery fiction and joined *Dime Detective*'s roster of contributors in 1935 with the first installment of his "Needle Mike" series. He brought the "Blue Barrel" to *Dime Detective* in 1936, but very few aficionados know that he didn't create the character for Ken White's popular pulp magazine.

A talented fictioneer who followed market trends closely and adapted to them readily, Barrett crashed the slick-paper market in 1939. With the exception of the odd story for *Argosy*, *Adventure*, or *Blue Book*, he spent the next several decades contributing fiction to the top-paying mainstream periodicals: *Colliers*, *Cosmopolitan*, *Good Housekeeping*, *Redbook*, and *The Saturday Evening Post*, among others. Two of his best-received novels, *The Left Hand of God* and *Lilies of the Field*, were made into movies (released in 1955 and 1963, respectively). He's little remembered today, even by pulp-fiction devotees, but he was a talented storyteller. I think you'll detect the early stirrings of that talent in "The Mobster Man," a product of his salad days.

Before I wrap things up, let me recommend the upcoming PulpFest, about which you can read in this issue's installment of "Convention Corner," and my new web site, muraniapress.com, which should be a regular and frequent destination of *BnT* readers. In addition to information about current and future issues of this magazine, you'll get the skinny on upcoming Murania Press books. I discuss related topics on a blog page, and there's a section where you can buy collectibles.

Finally, make sure your subscription is up to date, because the next issue—Summer 2012—is our big Tenth Anniversary number, and I can assure you it'll be something special. Keep monitoring the Murania Press web site for further details. *BnT*

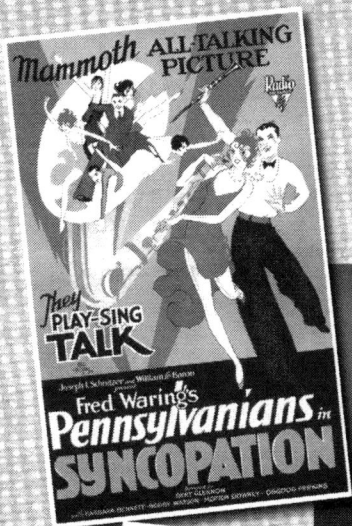

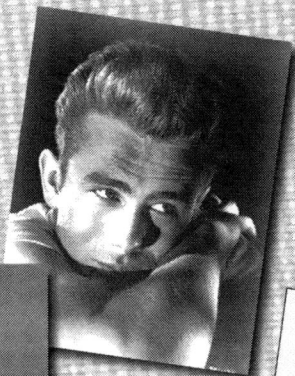

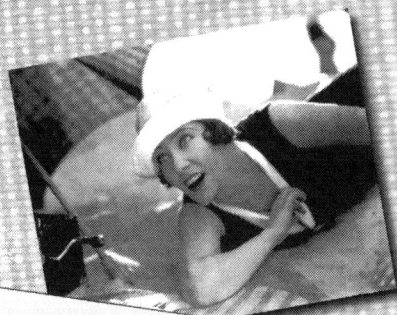

IN MEMORIAM

Glenn Lord
1931-2011

by Morgan Holmes

Once an author dies, interest in the writing generally wanes to the point that he or she is forgotten within a few years. This phenomenon may hold especially true for writers for the woodpulp magazines.

A few, such as Edgar Rice Burroughs or Frederick Faust, had novels published in hardback form after their initial magazine appearance. Movies were made. And eventually TV shows. In their lifetimes, their characters became entrenched in the culture: Tarzan. Destry. Dr. Kildare. John Carter of Mars.

For most pulp fictioneers, though, oblivion lurked right around the corner, almost as soon as they stopped writing. Some—L. Sprague de Camp, Hugh B. Cave, Manly Wade Wellman—kept the clock ticking longer by writing until the end of their long lives.

It is rare for a deceased writer to be figuratively resurrected and actually become bigger than during his or her pulp career. Behind these few rebirths are fans turned agent, editor, and even publisher, toiling to prevent obscurity from overtaking their favorite authors. August Derleth is a prime example for his work in preserving H. P. Lovecraft's writing. Francis M. Nevins is another, for his efforts to keep Cornell Woolrich from fading away.

One of the most astounding examples is that of Glenn Lord and his involvement with the legacy of Robert E. Howard—a writer who died at the age of 30, without seeing a single book published, and any kind of movie based on his work a mere pipe-dream. To think that, decades later, there would be a revival in paperbacks of the histori-

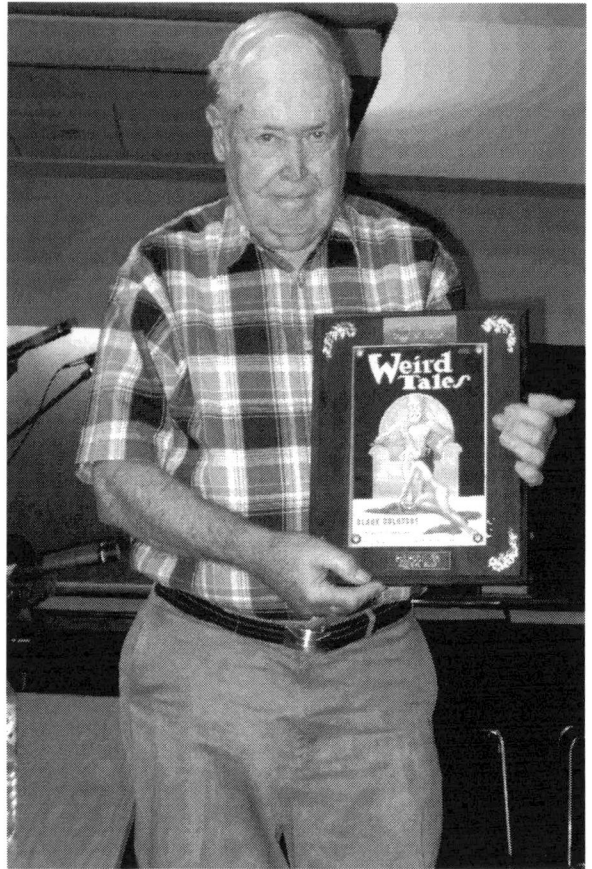

cal-adventure yarns, boxing stories, and Westerns—not to mention movies—of such an author is astounding.

Glenn Lord was born in Pelican, Louisiana when the Stock Market Crash of 1929 was hardening into the Great Depression. A reader of pulp magazines in the late 1940s, including *Planet Stories* and *Famous Fantastic Mysteries,* he discovered *The Avon Fantasy Reader* that reprinted Robert E. Howard stories. Starting in 1947, this digest reprint magazine introduced a new generation of readers to the Texas fictioneer. This new discovery also started Lord on the path of collecting issues of *Weird Tales.* He noticed an ad for the Arkham House book *Skull-Face and Others* in a book catalog and decided to order. It turned out

TALES OF CONAN

By Robert E. Howard and L. Sprague de Camp

He used to joke he was like the character Radar O'Reilly from the T.V. show *M.A.S.H.*

Gnome Press published Howard's "Conan the Cimmerian" stories during the 1950s in a series of volumes that was a modest success. Lord wanted to preserve Robert E. Howard's poetry in book form. His first foray as editor was collecting various poems—mostly from *Weird Tales*—for the book *Always Comes Evening.* He also obtained obscure Howard poems from Norris Chambers, a young neighbor and friend of Howard. A jacket cover was commissioned from artist Frank Utpatel, but the cost of printing and binding resulted in an unrealistic price for the book. August Derleth offered to publish *Always Comes Evening* as an Arkham House title. Lord paid the printing cost and was reimbursed from the proceeds.

The next project was *The Howard Collector,* starting in 1961. This was the first real Robert E. Howard small-press periodical. The issues were loaded with Howard's fiction, poetry, and letters. Reminiscences by people who knew Howard, such as E. Hoffmann Price and Tevis Clyde Smith, were also included. With issue #2 in 1962, some non-Robert E. Howard poetry was included, the first being a poem by Howard's Texas pal Tevis Clyde Smith. Newly written poetry became a feature of *The Howard Collector*, with new contributors including Walter Shedlofsky, Wade Wellman (Jr.), Kirk Mashburn, Richard L. Tierney, Lin Carter, and even L. Sprague de Camp! Howard-related poems by Emil Petaja and Robert Barlow that originally appeared in *Weird Tales* in the 1930s were also reprinted. Traditional heroic verse had been pretty much dead since the death of Howard. Glenn Lord resurrected it in his journal.

Remember Fritz Leiber's insightful essay on Robert E. Howard in *The Dark Barbarian*? The original version appeared in *The Howard Collector* as a series of three book reviews of the Lancer Conan paperbacks. We are all the richer for having those reviews delve into *why* the writ-

to be a life-changing experience, as he really liked this new author.

Robert E. Howard (1906-1936) was a writer for the pulp magazines, especially *Weird Tales* and *Action Stories* from 1925 to 1936. He is best remembered for creating the fantasy adventure hero, Conan of Cimmeria, in addition to Solomon Kane, King Kull, and Bran Mak Morn. Howard created an action-oriented form of heroic fantasy fiction that is called Sword-and-Sorcery. Howard was not limited to that one genre, also splashing the pulps with detective, Western, historical-adventure, horror, and boxing stories.

A stint in the U. S. Army interrupted Glenn's pulp collecting as he served in the Korean War, first in the artillery and then as company clerk.

ing of Robert E. Howard works so well. This was some of the first literary criticism ever done on Robert E. Howard, in the guise of a mere book review.

The Howard Collector lasted for 18 issues, the last dated Autumn 1973. Paul Herman has revived the publication, with one issue out in 2011 and another issue on the way.

An important event took place in 1965 when Lord tracked down the fabled trunk of Robert E. Howard. This treasure trove contained a mass of unpublished stories, fragments, synopses, and more. It had been lent to pulp writer and Howard friend E. Hoffmann Price, who then lent it to someone else until the whereabouts was unknown.

This act changed Howardian publishing profoundly. Instead of three King Kull stories and a poem in *Weird Tales*, there were now 12 stories and two fragments. The finding of the box unearthed another complete Conan story ("The Vale of Lost Women"), an almost-complete story ("Wolves Beyond the Border"), and four incomplete stories (some with synopses) and fragments that L. Sprague de Camp completed. Another fragment was turned into a story by Lin Carter ("The Hand of Nergal").

L. Sprague de Camp was a science-fiction writer whose origins go back to 1937 and the pulp magazine *Astounding Stories*. He had inserted himself as agent and posthumous collaborator for Robert E. Howard's Conan stories in the 1950s. He shopped around to get a deal with paperback publishers in the 1960s for Conan at a time that there was not an active agent for the copyright holders. Oscar J. Friend, agent for the Robert E. Howard copyright holders, had died and his daughter Kittie West decided to shut down the literary agent business in 1965. Based on his activities on the dead author's behalf, Glenn Lord got the job as the new agent.

In short order, he worked on getting Robert E. Howard out in paperback form. *King Kull* in 1967—everyone thinks Lin Carter edited it. No, it was Glenn Lord. Carter created stories out of

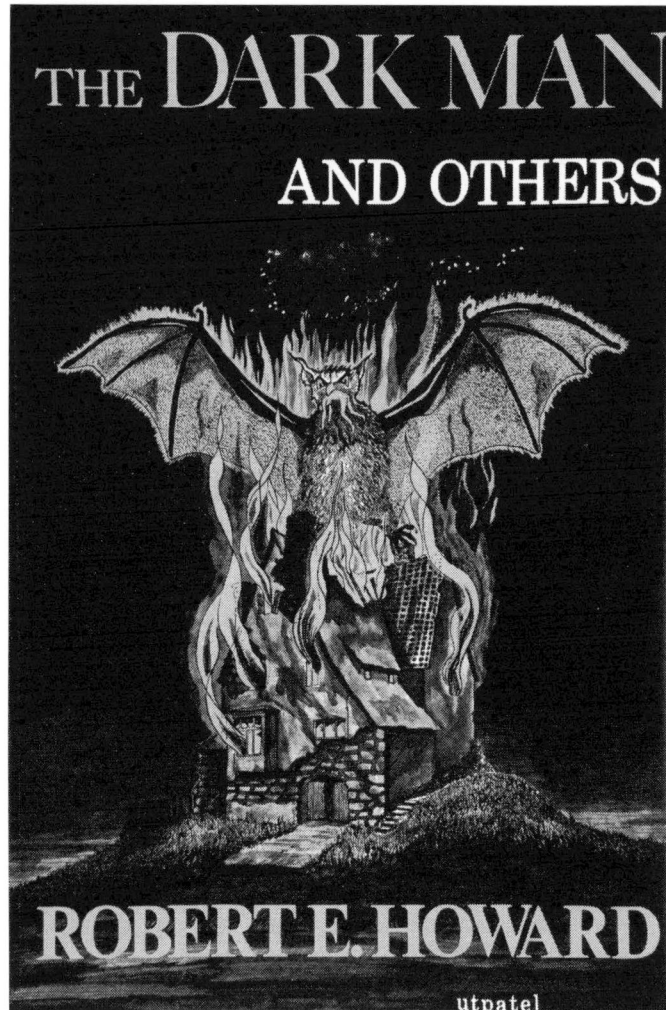

THE DARK MAN AND OTHERS

ROBERT E. HOWARD

utpatel

fragments and finished incomplete stories.

Wolfshead (Lancer Books, 1968) was the second paperback book Glenn Lord put together, making available some more obscure Robert E. Howard stories. *Bran Mak Morn* (Dell, 1969) was the third classic paperback bringing yet another Howard character to the masses. The Glenn Lord-edited paperbacks were a marked contrast to the L. Sprague de Camp-edited Conan paperbacks coming out at the same time. Glenn generally would use a Robert E. Howard letter as the introduction and eschew any self-aggrandizement, opinions, or half-baked posthumous psychoanalysis.

His long association with Donald M. Grant,

publisher of hardback books, began with *A Gent from Bear Creek* (1965) and resulted in a total of 31 books of Robert E. Howard prose and verse. In addition, Grant also published Lord's study of Howard, *The Last Celt*, a book that contained a mix of Robert E. Howard biography, bibliography, and miscellany.

When Lancer Books went down in bankruptcy, Glenn Lord made a deal with publisher Walter Zacharius' successor company, Zebra Books. Pretty much all the resulting collections—including *Tigers of the Sea, Black Vulmea's Vengeance,* and *The Vultures of Whapeton*—were put together by Glenn. Two books with Glenn's imprint stand out: *The Book of Robert E. Howard* (Zebra Books, 1976) and *The Second Book of Robert E. Howard* (Zebra Books, 1976). These were Robert E. Howard samplers that introduced readers to the wide range of Robert E. Howard—whether it was horror, historical, poetry, Western, weird menace, Sword-and-Sorcery, and so on. For each story Glenn Lord had short information-packed introductions that mentioned various pulp-magazine titles, editors, and fellow writers. When you read those books, you got a primer in pulp-magazine history.

After the Zebra Books deal, Glenn repeated the trick with Berkley Medallion. Some of the Berkley Medallion paperbacks had introductions by Gahan Wilson, Richard Lupoff, and another home run with Fritz Leiber in *Marchers of Valhalla.*

At the same time, Bantam Books published new editions of the *Wolfshead,* Kull, and Solomon Kane stories, as well as a paperback edition of *The Road of Azrael.*

What helped fuel these paperback anthologies was Glenn's willingness to deal with the small press. A steady number of unpublished stories made their way to publications such as *Fantasy Crossroads, Two-Gun Raconteur, Cross Plains*, and *The Howard Review.* Collections such as *The Last Ride* probably would not have happened if those yarns had not first appeared elsewhere. Robert E. Howard stories were also represented in such anthologies as *Horror Times Ten* (13 printings), *Thirteen Tales of Terror*, and *The Sixth Mayflower Book of Black Magic Stories.* Glenn made sure to constantly keep a steady stream of Robert E. Howard fiction available in one form or another.

Possibly the most important thing that Lord ever did was to make a deal for Marvel Comics to adapt Conan of Cimmeria into comic-book form. *Conan the Barbarian* started in 1970 and lasted for 275 issues. A magazine-sized black & white publication, *The Savage Sword of Conan*, lasted for 235 issues. This is what blew the doors wide open, enabling the most famous fictional barbarian to become a popular-culture icon. If you were a kid in the 1970s, more than likely you discovered Robert E. Howard through the pages of the Marvel comics. There would have been no Conan movies had there not first been a Conan comic book.

The explosion of Conan and Robert E. Howard in general helped fuel a Sword-and-Sorcery boom in the late 1970s. There was a period that when you went to the science-fiction section at a bookstore, you were likely to see as many barbarians as starships on paperback book covers. In the middle 1980s the Sword-and-Sorcery boom withered away as other forms of fantasy fiction came to the fore and dominated the market. Glenn Lord still managed to pull off one last book deal, licensing *The Robert E. Howard Library*, which was published by Baen Books in the middle 1990s.

Right after this transaction, Glenn Lord was let go as agent amidst infighting between the principals of Conan Properties, Inc., followed by an unwise lawsuit from the Howard copyright holders. The effect was immediate, as no Robert E. Howard was being reprinted in the late 1990s. Things were later patched up and Glenn once again acknowledged as the elder statesman of Howard fandom. He was a Guest of Honor at the 2006 Robert E. Howard Days celebration held at Cross Plains, Texas. A year later, he was honored at Pulpcon in Dayton, Ohio. During his last few years, friends and fans threw birthday parties for him at a favorite seafood restaurant.

Glenn Lord was fan, editor, publisher, and agent. Not many in this field can claim to achieve what he did in his lifetime. **BT**

CONVENTION CORNER

PulpFest 2012: Just Around the Corner

by the PulpFest Committee

It's that time again! With this year's Windy City convention now behind us, collectors of pulp magazines, vintage paperbacks, and other forms of popular fiction are looking forward to the fourth annual PulpFest, which promises to be the biggest and best yet.

The 2012 PulpFest will unfold from Thursday, August 9, through Sunday, August 12, at the Hyatt Regency Hotel in Columbus, Ohio. Yes, this is a new venue for us, and we're certain our attendees will be as delighted with it as we are. In addition to being a much better location—smack dab in the downtown area, surrounded by shops and restaurants within easy walking distance—the Hyatt has just completed a $12 million refurbishment. Want to check it out? Just check on the link at the top of our home page at pulpfest.com.

We have dual themes for this year's confab, and they involve two of the most famous and avidly collected authors in pop-culture history.

When readers of *The All-Story*, a Frank A. Munsey-published pulp magazine, picked up the magazine's February issue, they saw a cover featuring a sombrero-wearing Mexican framed in a window. Little did they realize that among the authors within was one who would soon rank among the leading producers of American popular fiction.

That *All-Story* for February 1912 featured a complete novel, ten short stories, and six serials, with "Under the Moons of Mars" listed above them all. The author of this "Romance of a soul astray," was listed as Norman Bean, a pen name for Edgar Rice Burroughs. Hiding behind a pseudonym in his initial effort as a professional writer, Burroughs would soon become one of the best-paid fictioneers to labor in the pulp market. Later that same year, the new author made an indelible mark on American pop culture with the appearance of "Tarzan of the Apes," published complete in the October issue of *The All-Story*.

To celebrate the 100th anniversary of the publication of "Under the Moons of Mars," better known by its book title *A Princess of Mars* and recently adapted to film as Disney's John Carter, PulpFest will devote a big chunk of its programming time to ERB's Barsoom series and related topics. For example, one of our panels is entitled "Pulp Visions of Mars." Among the participants will be PulpFest 2012's Guest of Honor, science-fiction writer Mike Resnick. Winner of five Hugo Awards and a Nebula Award, Mike first became involved in science fiction through the work of ERB. It's fitting, therefore, that our GoH is a veteran fan who, early in his pro career, "wanted nothing more than to write books in the style of Edgar Rice Burroughs."

Mike's first published work of science fiction, *The Forgotten Sea of Mars*, was a sequel to Burroughs' *Llana of Gathol*. After its release in 1965, Resnick transformed and expanded the story into *The Goddess of Ganymede* and its sequel *Pursuit on Ganymede*. Around the same time, Mike served as an associate editor of Camille Cazedessus' legendary fanzine *ERB-dom*.

Although Mike's later works did not necessarily reflect the influence of Edgar Rice Burroughs, he still appreciates the author's creations. In recent years, he has written introductions to new editions of *The Tarzan Twins* (Wildside Press), ERB's *The Land That Time Forgot* and Philip Jose Farmer's *Tarzan Alive* (both published by Bison Books). Currently, he is editing, with Bob Garcia, *The Worlds of Edgar Rice Burroughs*, an anthology of mostly original stories inspired by Burroughs and his creations. It will be published by Baen

Books and feature stories by Kevin J. Anderson, Joe Lansdale, Michael Moorcock, and others, as well as the first appearance of Resnick's "The Forgotten Sea of Mars" in nearly 50 years. We are honored by his presence at PulpFest and look forward to his participation in some of our special events.

Additionally, author-historian-artist David Saunders (son of famed pulp artist Norman Saunders), who has written extensively on the subject of illustration, will discuss J. Allen St. John, the artist perhaps most closely associated with the works of Edgar Rice Burroughs. David's research is impeccable and his knowledge of pulp art is unparalleled. His presentation will include a slide show featuring ERB-related works produced by St. John during his long association with the author.

Of course, the Mars and Tarzan centennials are not the only events that will make 2012 significant for PulpFest attendees: This year we also celebrate the 80th birthday of Conan the Cimmerian, the lusty barbarian who debuted in the December 1932 issue of the classic pulp magazine *Weird Tales*. Created by Robert E. Howard, Conan became a reader favorite and appeared in many stories over the next four years.

Although Howard died a suicide in 1936, his most famous creation was later revived in hardcover collections published by Arkham House and Gnome Press. But it was the mid-Sixties Lancer paperbacks, with their striking Frank Frazetta covers, that enthralled baby-boom readers, led to Conan movies and comic books, and gave rise to a new generation of Robert E. Howard scholars who have worked tirelessly to keep all their favorite author's works in print. (None more so than the late Glenn Lord, the subject of a tribute elsewhere in this issue of *BnT*.)

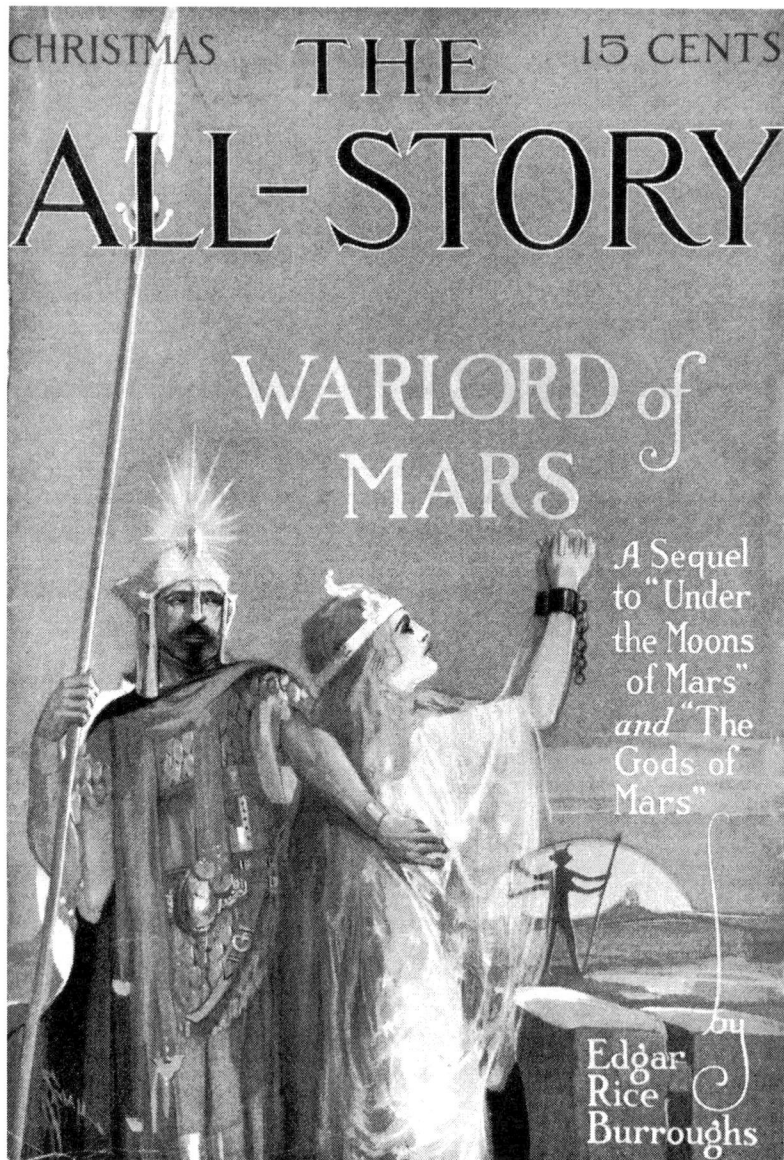

PulpFest will celebrate the Cimmerian's birthday and honor Howard's career with two very special programs. First, Rusty Burke will moderate a panel of REH experts who will discuss Conan, Howard's other characters, and the author's influence on the Sword-and-Sorcery genre. Rusty needs no introduction to devotees of "Two-Gun Bob." He is the editor of the highly acclaimed Howard reprint series published in the U. S. by Del Rey Books, the president of the Robert E. Howard

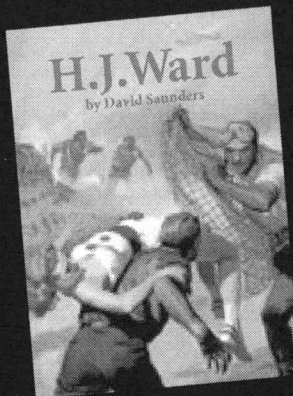

Foundation, and a long-time participant in *REHupa* (The Robert E. Howard United Press Association). We will provide the names of other panelists as soon as they are confirmed.

The second Conan-themed presentation will be made by another well-known Howard aficionado, Jim Keegan, who with his wife Ruth produces "The Adventures of Two-Gun Bob," which appears in every issue of *Conan, Kull*, and *Solomon Kane* published by Dark Horse Comics. The Keegans have also illustrated several of the Del Rey volumes (including *Crimson Shadows* and *Grim Land: The Best of Robert E. Howard, Volumes One & Two*) and are the proprietors of Jim & Ruth's Two-Gun Blog. Jim will offer a look at the Cimmerian as depicted by various illustrators over the last eight decades.

As we said above, Edgar Rice Burroughs and Robert E. Howard remain two of the most avidly collected pulp fictioneers, and we're certain that this year's PulpFest programs will win new fans for each. And that's just the beginning. We're already brainstorming ideas for other panels and presentations, so you can expect the same diverse mix of programming for which our convention has become famous. Check our website often for additional news.

PulpFest 2012 is now accepting registrations for attendees and table reservations for our hucksters. From the site's Registration page you'll be able to download our member and dealer registration forms, including ones that you can fill in and print from your own computer. You can pay for memberships and dealer tables through our Paypal Order page. You'll also be able to book a room at the Hyatt Regency Columbus at the convention rate of $109 plus tax by visiting our special link to the hotel. The entire process can be accomplished on line with the typing and some basic information and a few clicks of your computer mouse. But we're also happy to accommodate those of you who prefer filling out paper forms and sending them through the mail with checks.

If you're among the few *BnT* readers who don't know what PulpFest is, or why it's a must-attend event for people with our interests, visit pulpfest.com to see reviews and blog entries pertaining to our first three outings. We even have a pulp-history primer for newbies!

Regular PulpFest attendees always look forward to getting their copies of *The Pulpster*, our combination of fanzine and program book. This publication—actually, "institution" would be a better word—was first issued two decades ago at Pulpcon, the summer pulp show that PulpFest supplanted. Well, 2012 marks another milestone besides those mentioned above: after 21 years at *The Pulpster*'s helm, editor Tony Davis plans to call it quits. Therefore, he and designer Bill Lampkin are pulling out all of the stops to make this year's issue the most memorable issues of the entire run. All members of PulpFest 2012 receive a complimentary copy of *The Pulpster*, and leftover copies can be purchased from us after the convention for five dollars each.

If you'd like to place an ad in this year's *Pulpster*, there's still time to do so. However, the May 31st deadline is fast approaching. Our rates are very reasonable: color back cover and inside color covers cost $125; full pages cost $65, half-pages $40 and quarter pages $25. Print specifications, payment information, and more can be found on the Program Book page of our website. To inquire about space availability, please write to Jack Cullers at jack@pulpfest.com. *The Pulpster* has a circulation of approximately 500 copies. All advertising is sold on a first-come, first-served basis, with payment expected immediately after reserving space.

Another way to advertise at PulpFest is to donate material for our giveaway table. Over the years, *The Magazine of Fantasy and Science Fiction*, *Book Source Magazine*, Girasol Collectables, Engle Publishing, and other organizations have donated publications that were given away free to PulpFest attendees. Your donation will be acknowledged on our website and at the convention. If you'd like to offer something for our giveaway table, please contact Barry Traylor at barry@pulpfest.com.

Plan today on attending PulpFest. Whether you're an experienced fan or just a green newbie, we can promise you a good time. Our dealers and attendees are great people, and nobody leaves their first PulpFest without making new friends! **BnT**

TRICKS OF THE TRADE

Improving the Detective Novel

(*Writer's Digest,* January 1941)

by Frank Gruber

Digest editor's note: The author of The French Key, The Talking Clock, *and* The Laughing Fox *reveals another trade secret.*

The past year saw four Gruber mystery novels (under Frank's own name) come out of the binder's press. Most "bestseller" lists of the year contained one or more of the amazing Mr. Gruber's books. We say amazing because it was only six years ago that this Digest *subscriber hopefully came East from Mt. Morris, Illinois, and just five years ago that his hotel locked him out because of you-know-what. Since then, Frank Gruber has only gone up. His publishers, Farrar and Rinehart, are putting big money advertising behind his titles, and we look to see Frank Gruber pass the $20,000 bracket this year.*

A year ago, Frank Gruber told you in the Digest *how he analyzed the mystery novel before he wrote his own first book,* The French Key. *The article was printed before the book was published. The book itself went through two printings within two weeks of publication. William Lyon Phelps wrote a letter to the publishers, F&R, saying: "*The French Key *is one of the very best of 8000 mysteries I have read."*

Six months after the publication of The French Key, *F&R brought out Gruber's second mystery,* The Laughing Fox, *and the critics went on parade. F&R signed Gruber for eight additional mystery novels to be published during the next two years.*

Gruber is keeping up with his short fiction, in both slicks and pulps. His career, though more luminous than many, follows the well-carved path of sincere, hard-working writers who have made good use of the pages of the Digest, *and now return the compliment.*

"The Man's a Mad Dog" — CADDO CAMERON

ShortStories

November 10th

25¢

Some clever stuff in a Kappie De Vries novelette
by
R. V. GERY

Beginning a new mystery serial
The French Key
by
FRANK GRUBER

H S POTTER

The manager of the Westover Hotel wrote a letter to Steve Fisher: "We have had several complaints about the large animal in your room and we regret we must request you, etc., etc."

This "large animal" is the biggest, hungriest Great Dane you ever saw in your life. When Steve, who writes those yarns for *Cosmopolitan, Liberty, The Post,* etc., went to France a couple of years ago he took this small horse with him. He brought him back to New York and then traveled with him to Hollywood and back once more.

This far-traveled Great Dane can inhale three or four pounds of hamburger in a couple of gulps.

I am going to reveal to those readers of *Writer's Digest* through an incident that came to me

LEFT: Frank Gruber's "The French Key" was serialized in *Short Stories* prior to hardcover publication.

BELOW: This 1939 Paramount mystery was based on one of Gruber's "Oliver Quade" stories.

because of Steve's Dane, the most important thing I have learned about writing a mystery novel.

I refer to the matter of invention. You may call it situation or incident.

The manager of a large bookstore gave me an advance copy of a mystery novel by a new author and asked me for my honest opinion of the story. I read it with more care than I usually read a book.

It started off swell. The detective was a colorful character. The writing had a vitality you seldom find, the dialog was crisp and the story moved. It lacked only two things, but those two things meant all the difference between an outstanding mystery and "just another mystery novel."

The story lacked a theme and it lacked invention. All right, nine out of ten mystery novels lack those two very same things. That's why they sell their 2000 to 3000 copies and are forgotten. A dozen or so mysteries stand out every year from 500 that are published. In practically every case these outstanding mysteries have both theme and invention.

In a previous article in the *Writer's Digest* I stated my opinion that a colorful theme was vital in a best-selling mystery novel. I still hold that to be true, but now I add that without invention the theme falls flat.

My readers—both of them—know what I mean by a theme, so I'm not going to harp on that again. (A theme is simply the same tune running through your book. For example, my book *The Laughing Fox* is all about silver foxes; the theme is silver foxes. My current mystery novel, *The Talking Clock*, has to do with clocks.)

I am going to speak about invention, and refer again to the book by the new author, who shall remain nameless. The background of the story is a big city and the story shifts from office, to apartment dwelling, to a nightclub, and then makes the rounds again. Various murders are committed and there are several suspects. The hero moves through it all, is suspected of the murders, and finally saves himself by pinning the rap on the real culprit. That is all there is to the story and I will defy you to distinguish it from any one of a hundred mystery novels you've read.

That is exactly why this story falls flat on its appendix. It has nothing different in it, nothing unusual. It lacks both theme and invention.

To illustrate this thing I call invention I submit to you now the somewhat detailed plot of a mystery novel that contains invention in copious quantities.

Two itinerant book salesmen named Johnny Fletcher and Sam Cragg are locked out of their hotel room for non-payment of rent. It is night

DEATH OF A CHAMPION

LYNNE OVERMAN
VIRGINIA DALE
JOSEPH ALLEN, Jr.
DONALD O'CONNOR
SUSAN PALEY
ROBERT PAIGE

Screen Play by Stuart Palmer and Cortland Fitzsimmons
Directed by Robert Florey · A Paramount Picture

The Full Savor of a Salted Mine in Nevada Comes Out in New York's Theatrical District

CONCLUSION

THE FRENCH KEY

By FRANK GRUBER

and raining bulldogs and Siamese cats. Suspecting that such a thing might happen to them, the boys have supplied themselves with the key of an adjoining room and entering it step from the window ledge to the window of their own locked room. They force entrance and then discover a dead man on their bed. In his hand is a five-dollar gold piece. While they are appropriating it a telephone rings and a voice warns them to leave the room immediately. Panic-stricken, they turn to the window and to their chagrin discover that the occupant of the adjoining room, through which they made ingress, has returned.

All this in the first chapter. Being locked out of a hotel room may not be particularly novel, but to make entrance to their room in the manner described gives a fresh twist to the situation. The discovery of the dead man in the locked room presents a problem. How did he get there? Certainly the hotel management looked inside before locking the room. Then the gold coin . . . and the mysterious telephone call . . . and their retreat cut off. That's complication piled on complication and it adds up to invention.

Continue now with their escape, a forced one, over the protests of the occupant of the adjoining room and then, once safe, the discovery that the five dollar gold piece has the date 1822 on it and is the rarest gold coin in existence, worth ten thousand dollars.

In the morning they take the coin to a rare-coin dealer, who reacts to it in a peculiar manner. Continue at a more moderate pace to the estate of a wealthy man, where there are three iron lawn monstrosities in the shape of bears. To demonstrate his strength, Sam Cragg lifts one of the bears, but he is unable to lift another of equal size.

That night one of the iron bears disappears. It is mysteriously returned later.

Pursued by the police, dodging several persons who have shown an extraordinary interest in the valuable gold piece and made fantastic offers for it, and on the verge of being arrested, Johnny Fletcher drops the coin into a telephone coin-box.

Apparently gone for good, another murder is

committed and the gold coin reappears in the corpse's hand. Why? How?

While all this is going on, Johnny Fletcher repairs his financial circumstances by a couple of rather startling bits of chicanery. Invention.

Turned away at the gates of an estate, Fletcher hires a colored orchestra, blacks his own face, then piles into a gaudily painted car with the musicians and an assortment of drums, bass viols, saxophones, etc. Could you pick out a black-faced white man from that conglomeration?

Fletcher needs a used car. His method of buying one is novel, to say the least.

I'll stop here on this particular plot, lest I bore. I'll go back to Steve Fisher and his "large animal." I mentioned that the sight of this dog consuming about four pounds of hamburger was something to behold. Watching him do this disappearing act one time, an idea struck me. Suppose Johnny Fletcher and Sam Cragg, those two perpetually broke book salesmen, should be burdened with not one big dog, but 200?

A mystery novel, *The Hungry Dog*, was the result.

Sam Cragg's uncle has died and left him his entire estate. The estate consists of 200 St. Bernard dogs. The boys spend their last dollar getting to the place, not knowing what the inheritance consists of. The first thing they're presented with is a bill for $1800 for dog food and a notice that unless it is paid no more dog meat will be forthcoming. A murder is committed and things begin to pop . . . and all the time the dogs are getting hungrier and hungrier.

Don't worry, dog lovers, we fed the 200 St. Bernards. How? By invention.

Hotel managers who lock out guests just because they can't pay their rent are pretty nasty individuals. Things should happen to them. Johnny Fletcher's main mission in life is to mete out justice to such hotel managers. He's badly in need of a suit of clothes and by accident learns the name of the clothing store where the manager is accustomed to buying his suits.

Disguising his voice he telephones the store and tells them that he's just spilled a bottle of ink on his new suit and to please rush over another, measurements of which they have. A messenger boy is naturally sent with the package and Johnny meets him in the lobby of the hotel. He is hatless and wearing a white carnation and since he accosts the messenger, the latter naturally assumes that he is the manager and hands over the parcel. The hotel manager will be surprised on the first of the month when he gets a bill for a suit of which he knows nothing.

However, to make things a little more interesting, the clothing store people, in their haste, neglected to include the extra pair of trousers and they send it over at a time when Johnny isn't in the lobby. The manager learns the awful truth . . . and matches the extra pair of trousers with the brand new suit Fletcher is wearing.

Your detective sits around in a night club and drinks dry martinis and Old Fashioneds and double Scotches and he makes smart cracks at sleek villains and gin-swizzling blondes and he goes out and gets cracked on the noggin and busts a few skulls himself. He jaws with the cops and asks questions. He does this for two hundred and some pages, going from penthouse to gin mill and back to the penthouse, and on page 291 he finally says: "Bledsoe, you're the lug who gave them the business and they're warming up the hot seat for you."

> Every detective-story writer has to work from his skeleton plot. The dressing he gives it is what makes his story different from other detective stories.

You write this story and I don't care how clever your dialog is, how marvelous your writing, your book will get nice, polite reviews and sell between 2000 and 3000 copies and in a month no one will remember it.

All detective stories have the same basic plot. A murder plot is committed, perhaps two or three; questions are asked and answered and your detective makes certain deductions and eventually pins the guilt upon the culprit.

Every detective-story writer has to work from his skeleton plot. The dressing he gives it is what makes his story different from other detective stories. But too often this dressing is commonplace. The jaded detective story reader has read essentially the same thing a hundred times. Murder in itself is no longer startling or unusual.

That is why the smart detective-story writer gives his story invention.

In my own case, I try to have a minimum of six or seven inventions in a novel and I try to space them out so there'll be one every two or three chapters.

In *The Talking Clock*, all the characters are introduced in the first two chapters. A murder is committed in the third and my detective heroes, Johnny Fletcher and Sam Cragg, become fugitives and are fervently pursued by John Law. This pursuit is rather a lengthy one—consuming altogether about three chapters. But after a chapter or so I could see that the reader might become somewhat impatient so I injected one of these things I call an invention.

Hungry and in desperate financial straits, the boys are walking past a theater that is playing Walt Disney's *Pinocchio*. A man steps out from under the marquee and asks them if they want to earn two dollars apiece for a day's work. Naturally, they snatch at the opportunity. And then . . . they discover that they are required to don *Pinocchio* outfits and dance and prance in front of the theatre. It's a publicity stunt for the theater, intended to attract crowds—and it worked very well in New York, where it was actu-

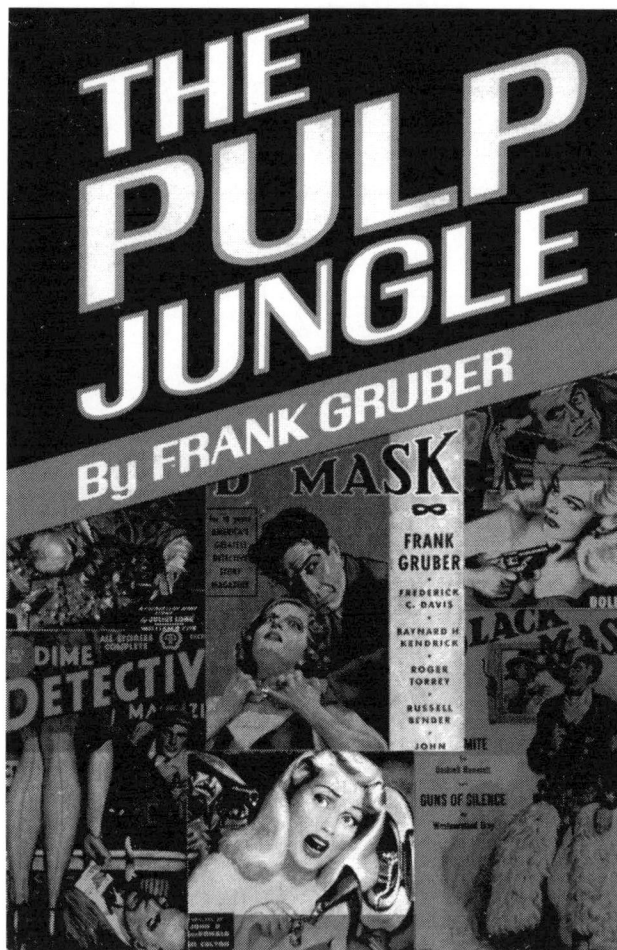

ally pulled through the lengthy run of the picture.

This *Pinocchio* episode was worked into my story as an integral part of the plot. It broke the monotony of the chase and it alleviated, to a certain extent, the financial condition of Johnny Fletcher and Sam Cragg.

There are other inventions in *The Talking Clock*. They come at proper intervals. Whenever the story is in danger of lagging through routine, although necessary, detective stuff, *bang!* comes an invention.

If you have a good theme and invention your book will sell a good many more than 3000 copies and it will be still selling a year after publication. And when your second book comes out it'll take up where the first one left off.　　**BNT**

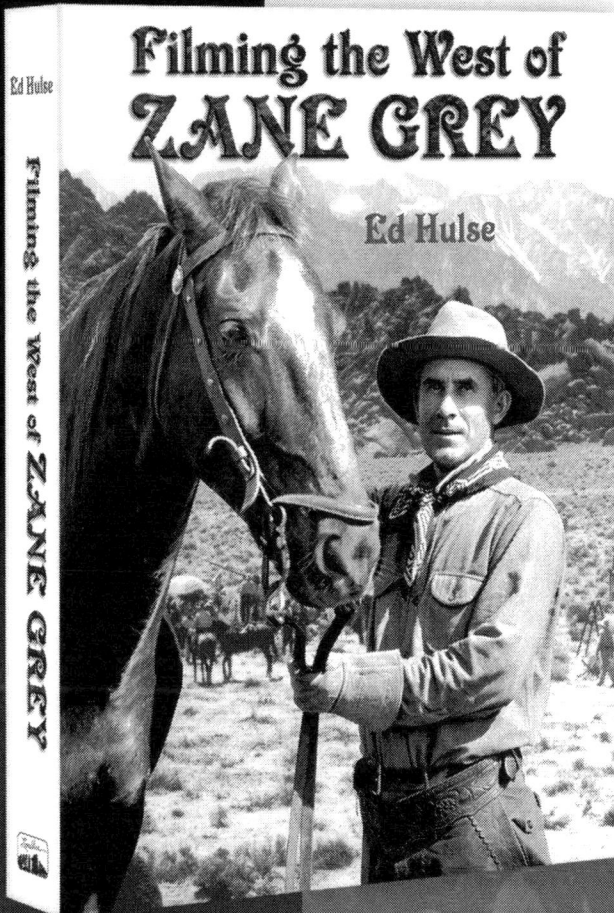

CLIFFHANGER CLASSICS

The Shadow

by Ed Hulse

Harry Cohn's Columbia Pictures Corporation was a late player in the serial game, coming to bat in 1937 after various independent producers had departed the field for good. With only Universal and Republic as competition, the studio initially outsourced chapter-play production to the father-son team of Louis and Adrian Weiss, whose Artclass Pictures had long been a mainstay of Poverty Row. Their three serials for Columbia—*Jungle Menace*, *The Mysterious Pilot*, and *The Secret of Treasure Island*—were undistinguished efforts that underperformed in the marketplace. Cohn summarily dismissed Weiss *pere et fils*, assigning newly hired producer Jack Fier to oversee *The Great Adventures of Wild Bill Hickok*, previously announced as the fourth Weiss/Columbia serial of the 1937-38 season.

Fier determined that the only effective way to seize serial market share was to keep Columbia's chapter-play production in house and make the studio's episodic epics on a slightly grander scale than originally contemplated. This, presumably, would make them more appealing to exhibitors previously reliant on Universal and Republic product.

Columbia's four 1938-39 serials—led by *The Spider's Web*, an action-packed adaptation of the Popular Publications hero pulp that was *The Shadow Magazine*'s most serious competitor— enjoyed considerable box-office success but failed to return the expected margin of profit because their production costs were so high. At a time when the average Republic and Universal serial cost $150,000 to $175,000, Fier was spending well over $200,000 for each of his. Since exhibitor rentals averaged five dollars per chapter at this time, the extra expenditures cut into Columbia's revenues.

The somewhat more lavishly appointed Fier-produced chapter plays did, however, secure enough bookings and generate enough favorable publicity to solidify the studio's position in this niche market. But, having accomplished this aim, Harry Cohn retrenched by once again outsourcing serial production, this time to Larry Darmour, who for some years had been supplying Columbia with short subjects and B-grade Westerns on an independent basis. Cohn and Fier were gambling that serial production quality was secondary to promotional value: With an exhibitor client base established, it would be just as easy to sell the studio's chapter plays based on the presence of marketable stars or popular characters licensed from other mediums.

It fell to Jack Fier to select properties with appeal to the generally youthful audience that patronized serials. This meant securing screen rights to characters from pulps, comics, and radio shows. With Darmour hired to produce four chapter plays per "season" (in those days, a movie "season" began sometime after Labor Day and extended through Spring to the beginning of Summer, which typically saw a reduction in theatergoing), Fier commenced his licensing efforts.

The all-important season-opening slot had been reserved for a serial built around some popular fictional character. Following negotiations with Street & Smith, Columbia on May 26, 1939 paid $7000 for the right to produce one motion picture, either a 15-episode serial or a long feature film, based on The Shadow. Surviving documents reveal that the publishing company's vp/general manager Henry W. "Bill" Ralston and

The Shadow

1940 Columbia

Stars: Victor Jory, Veda Ann Borg, Roger Moore

"THE SHADOW"
HOT FROM RADIO AND MAGAZINE!
VICTOR JORY
VEDA ANN BORG • ROGER MOORE • ROBERT FISKE
BASED UPON STORIES PUBLISHED IN "THE SHADOW" MAGAZINE
SCREEN PLAY BY JOSEPH POLAND • NED DANDY • JOSEPH O'DONNELL
JAMES W. HORNE
A COLUMBIA CHAPTER PLAY

COLUMBIA PICTURES CORPORATION
OF CALIFORNIA, LTD.
1438 GOWER STREET
HOLLYWOOD, CALIFORNIA
HOLLYWOOD 3181

July 19, 1939

Street & Smith Publications, Inc.
79 Seventh Avenue
New York, N. Y.

Gentlemen:

Reference is hereby made to the Agreement between us, dated
May 26, 1939, whereby we acquired the right to make one serial
motion picture to be based upon any or all of the literary
works mentioned in Schedules "A" and "B" attached to said
Agreement.

Please be advised that we do hereby elect to acquire the
motion picture rights to the following literary works:

                    FROM SCHEDULE "A"
        THE GREEN HOODS - Published August 15, 1938
        SILVER SKULL   -   "   January 1, 1939
        THE LONE TIGER -   "   February 15,1939

                    FROM SCHEDULE "B"
        PRELUDE TO TERROR - January 29, 1939

We are giving you this notice in accordance with the provisions
of Article I of the above mentioned Agreement, dated May 26, 1939.

                            Very truly yours,

                            COLUMBIA PICTURES CORPORATION

                            By _____
                                    Vice President

LEFT: Columbia Pictures memo asking Street & Smith for rights to specific Shadow stories.

BELOW: The Shadow (Victor Jory) aids Margot (Veda Ann Borg), who is menaced by Flint (Jack Ingram).

licensing director William de Grouchy exercised great care in crafting the agreement and insisted the filmmakers maintain fidelity to Street & Smith's most profitable pulp hero.

Significantly, however, the deal permitted Columbia to adapt episodes of the radio show as well as novels printed in the magazine. This was a potentially risky concession because the two versions of The Shadow were fundamentally incompatible. In a July 19 letter to the publishing company, Columbia vice president B. B. Kahane informed Street & Smith that the studio had decided to use as source material "The Green Hoods" (published in the August 15, 1938 issue), "Silver Skull" (January 1, 1939), and "The Lone Tiger" (February 15, 1939). He also requested a copy of the script to one of the radio episodes, "Prelude to Terror" (broadcast January 29, 1939).

Apparently, Fier at first intended to produce the Shadow serial in house. Brief news items published in movie-industry trade papers during the early part of summer reported that Lorna Gray would take the female lead, and that Norman Deming and D. Ross Lederman would direct in tandem. As all were under contract to Columbia, these accounts lend credence to the supposition that the chapter play was initially slated for more extravagant production mounting along the lines of *The Spider's Web*. But when Larry Darmour signed on to supply serials for Columbia distribution the property was assigned to him.

Writers Joseph F. Poland and Ned Dandy, who had collaborated on the previous two Fier-produced serials, teamed with accomplished scripter Joseph O'Donnell to devise a story containing 15 episodes of thrills that could be realized cinematically on short money. (They were assisted by Charles Condon and John Thomas Neville, whose contributions could not have been substantial as they did not receive screen credit.) Reportedly, Darmour's Columbia chapter plays were budgeted at $100,000—less than half what Fier had been spending. Speed and economy became the new watchwords of

Columbia's serial unit. Sound-stage scenes would be shot at Larry Darmour's studio on Santa Monica Boulevard in Hollywood. Exterior street scenes would be taken in Burbank at what was called the Columbia Ranch, or on the adjoining Warner Brothers back lot, access to which was available for a modest rental fee. The screenwriters kept cost limitations very much in mind as they concocted the scenario, and by mid-July a first draft had already been completed.

Of course, helming production of action-packed, highly melodramatic serials required a master's touch, so at Fier's suggestion Darmour hired James W. Horne, who had co-directed *The Spider's Web* and *Flying G-Men*. Although Horne was best known for his comedies, including many shorts and features starring Laurel & Hardy, he directed numerous chapter plays in the silent era, among them *Bull's Eye* (1917) and *Hands Up!* (1918), which had made top box-office stars of their respective stars, Eddie Polo and Ruth Roland.

The casting process yielded mixed results, although Darmour scored a coup by landing highly regarded major-studio player Victor Jory for the lead role. Actually, Darmour didn't make the deal himself. Canadian-born Jory had been working for Columbia off and on since 1934, and he enjoyed a good relationship with the notoriously irascible Harry Cohn. Even though the darkly handsome, vaguely sinister-looking actor had played leads before, he found steadier work in character parts and in 1939 was considered one of Hollywood's top heavies. His film work that year had already included high-profile villain portrayals in *Dodge City* and *Gone with the Wind.*

"My agent told me he'd made a two-picture deal for me at Columbia," Jory recalled to me in a 1980 interview. "Harry Cohn threw me into [the serial]. He said, 'Vic, you're going to be The Shadow.' It was as simple as that."

The serial's storyline combined elements of both pulp magazine and radio show, although it naturally leaned toward the former, as contractually obligated. The chief element borrowed from The Shadow's airwave adventures was Margot Lane, played by blonde, brassy Veda Ann Borg, a former Warner Brothers starlet most frequently seen as a gangster's moll or wisecracking showgirl. Borg lost her berth at Warners following a serious car accident in which she suffered serious facial injuries after being thrown through the windshield. Darmour had used her previously in a Bill Elliott Western, *The Law Comes to Texas* (1939), and she agreed to do the Shadow serial while waiting for another round of plastic sur-

gery. Since she still bore facial scars Veda had to be made up, lit and photographed carefully, so she received very few close-ups. A talented actress, Borg was nonetheless ill suited to play the glamorous, sophisticated Margot depicted in the radio series.

Rounding out the starring trio was one Roger Moore, cast as The Shadow's chief aide, Harry Vincent. Moore was in fact Joe Young, the older brother of second-tier movie star and TV's future Marcus Welby, Robert Young. Joe's career had never really taken off, and the role of Vincent was the last sizable one he got. Although he continued to work well into the Fifties, after *The Shadow* the elder Young most frequently appeared in uncredited bit parts. Also seen as familiar figures from the pulp magazine were veteran character actors Frank LaRue, playing Commissioner Ralph Weston, and Edward Peil, as Inspector Joe Cardona.

Principal photography began in the fall of 1939—the exact date is unknown—and proceeded at a rapid clip. "We did 15 episodes in 30 days," said Jory years later. "Less, actually, because we didn't shoot on Sundays. It was hard work—early mornings, late nights, a lot of rushing around." The Fier-produced serials, by contrast, had consumed six to eight weeks of shooting time.

Horne impressed upon his actors a need for speed and didn't waste any time on the niceties of staging scenes. "He instructed us very quickly," Jory remembered. "No real direction in terms of performances, except that we had to take everything 'big' [with exaggerated reactions]. He'd sketch the where and how of a scene, and give us the basic attitude of it, but mostly it was a question of hitting the marks and delivering the lines on cue. We did damn few retakes, and only then if there had been a problem with camera or sound. On serials you didn't get multiple takes to experiment with different line readings."

While shooting *The Shadow*, Horne introduced another time-saving innovation to shave hours off the schedule. In those days, fight scenes were

LEFT: A henchman (Constantine Romanoff) seems unnerved by the Black Tiger's instructions.

BELOW: Glenn Cravath's watercolor rough for a banner advertising the serial, scanned from the original art.

always shot twice—once in a "master" shot that took in the whole set and covered the melee from beginning to end, then with a series of shorter, closer shots that sometimes showed the principals throwing punches, rather than their stunt doubles. These "insert" shots would be cut into the masters to quicken the scene's pace and further the illusion that the actors were doing their own fighting.

George DeNormand, an experienced stuntman who doubled Victor Jory in *The Shadow*, explained to me in 1973 that Horne came up with a way to avoid the time-consuming process of relighting the set for close-ups and refitting it with duplicates of props that had been damaged or destroyed in the first take. "Instead of shooting the scene twice," said DeNormand, "[Horne] got actors who could do their own fights and used them as the heavies. Then he set up two cameras, side by side. One camera took the master shot from a fixed position. The other was tricked out with a special lens that would give you a closer view. The second operator was told to follow me around the set [by swiveling the camera]. This way, the director could chop up the second-unit footage to get those quick, close cuts he needed to edit into the master shot, without having to set everything up a second time. There was never a worry I'd be recognized in the closer view because I was wearing the hat and the cape and a little strip mask that covered the bottom half of my face."

Horne used this technique sparingly in *The Shadow* but more extensively in the following nine Columbia chapter plays he directed for Larry Darmour. (For the subsequent serials DeNormand was replaced as lead double by Eddie Parker and, in the Western cliffhangers, by Cliff Lyons.) Cinematographer James S. Brown Jr. and his assistant "undercranked" fight scenes to speed up the action, making the brawls seem more furious but also giving them a Keystone Kops aspect that latter-day viewers find risible. In a way, though, that was intentional. While directing his Darmour serials Horne never fully sublimated his comedic leanings.

For reasons unknown, *The Shadow* had a national release date of January 5, 1940, several months later than the typical season-opening serial. Street & Smith promoted the film extensively, mentioning it several times in the magazine's "Highlights on The Shadow" department and some of the company's other pulps. The chapter play's theatrical playoff period coincided with an increased effort to market the character; 1940 saw the marketing of numerous licensed products and multi-media spin-offs. Fans could buy Shadow hats, masks, cloaks, board games, make-up kits, gun-and-holster sets, and other paraphernalia tangentially connected to the Master of Darkness. Street & Smith launched a Shadow comic book in March of 1940, and a newspaper strip syndicated by the Ledger Syndicate followed shortly thereafter.

fight against crime: Lin Chang, a shifty Chinese merchant with underworld ties, and The Shadow, a mystery man whose hat, cloak, and sinister laugh were trademarks instantly recognizable to evildoers everywhere.

The Black Tiger's identity was a closely guarded secret: Not even his own men know who the Tiger really was, because he possessed the power of invisibility and transmitted instructions to the gang, sight unseen, through a wood-mounted tiger head outfitted with glowing eyes and radio speaker. But as the serial progressed it became apparent that he was one of the industrialists who met regularly with Cranston and Commissioner Weston at the Cobalt Club.

Week after week, The Shadow fought the Black Tiger to a standstill, nearly losing his life at the close of each episode only to escape miraculously at the beginning of the next. The chapter-ending perils lacked ingenuity; an inordinate number of installments closed with a ceiling collapsing on the fallen, unconscious Shadow— who groggily disengaged himself from the wreckage and staggered away the following week.

Truth be told, *The Shadow* didn't follow the pulp magazine or radio show as closely as it did *The Spider's Web*. In fact, it's fair to assume that screenwriters Dandy, Poland, and O'Donnell were instructed to copy the earlier serial, a box-office smash that single-handedly made Columbia a force to reckon with in the chapter-play market. The similarities are marked: *The Shadow*'s Lamont Cranston, like *Web*'s Richard Wentworth, is identified as a scientific criminologist rather than as the wealthy dilettante and world traveler he is in Walter Gibson's stories. The Lin Chang identity corresponds with no character in the Shadow saga but performs the same narrative function as Wentworth's Blinky McQuade persona. Likewise, the serial's Harry Vincent doesn't act independently, as he generally does in the pulp yarns; he stays close to The Shadow in the manner of Wentworth's aides Jackson and Ram Singh.

Moreover, *The Shadow* utilizes the same plot

Of course, buying a comic book or board game wasn't nearly as exciting as seeing one's favorite character live on the big screen, and Columbia's *Shadow* packed houses with devotees of radio show and pulp magazine alike. Serial fans huddled in darkened theaters all across the country learned in Chapter One, "The Doomed City," that the economic life of a great metropolis was being threatened by a well-organized criminal body headed by a mysterious figure known as the Black Tiger, whose mad ambition was to acquire "supreme financial power." To this end he waged a systematic campaign of terrorization and destruction—blowing up factories, crashing trains and planes, extorting money from fear-paralyzed tycoons.

The city's captains of industry prevailed upon Lamont Cranston (described as a "noted scientist and criminologist") to help combat the Tiger and his minions. Unbeknownst to them, Cranston had created two separate personalities to further his as *The Spider's Web.* Both serials posit the existence of a deranged mastermind who employs an army of henchmen to terrorize industrial leaders in a bid for economic control of a major city. Both show the police powerless to stem the tide of terror resulting from heedless destruction of life and property, concentrated on modes of transportation and newly invented devices.

The writers didn't entirely ignore the Shadow of pulp and radio. The serial is littered with bits and pieces of the licensed material. For example, the master villain's name and a courtroom scene in Chapter One are clearly inspired by "The Lone Tiger." The opening installment's climax, in which exploding light bulbs (!) are set off by a sudden surge of current, is adapted from "Prelude to Terror." A Chapter Two sequence, in which a disguised Shadow enters the Black Tiger's lair by donning one of the full-face masks worn by the villain's henchmen during meetings with their leader, was clearly inspired by a similar episode in "The Green Hoods."

The chapter play's scripters mined several plot nuggets from "Silver Skull." For example, one scene from that novel finds The Shadow trapped in an underground chamber and taunted by the mystery villain, who speaks through a life-sized mechanical skull outfitted with a radio speaker. While taunting his enemy, Silver Skull fills the room with gas—which, ignited by sparks, causes an explosion that brings the roof crashing down on The Shadow, who narrowly escapes. Poland, Dandy, and O'Donnell got *two* cliffhanger endings out of that one Walter Gibson-devised incident. Other "Silver Skull" elements employed in *The Shadow* include the systematic kidnapping of wealthy and powerful men and the repeated destruction of airplanes by mysterious means.

Aside from Margot's presence and the aforementioned bit with the exploding light bulbs, the serial took nothing from the Shadow radio show. Darmour and company made a reasonable effort to ensure that followers of the pulp Shadow would recognize their hero on screen. (In this

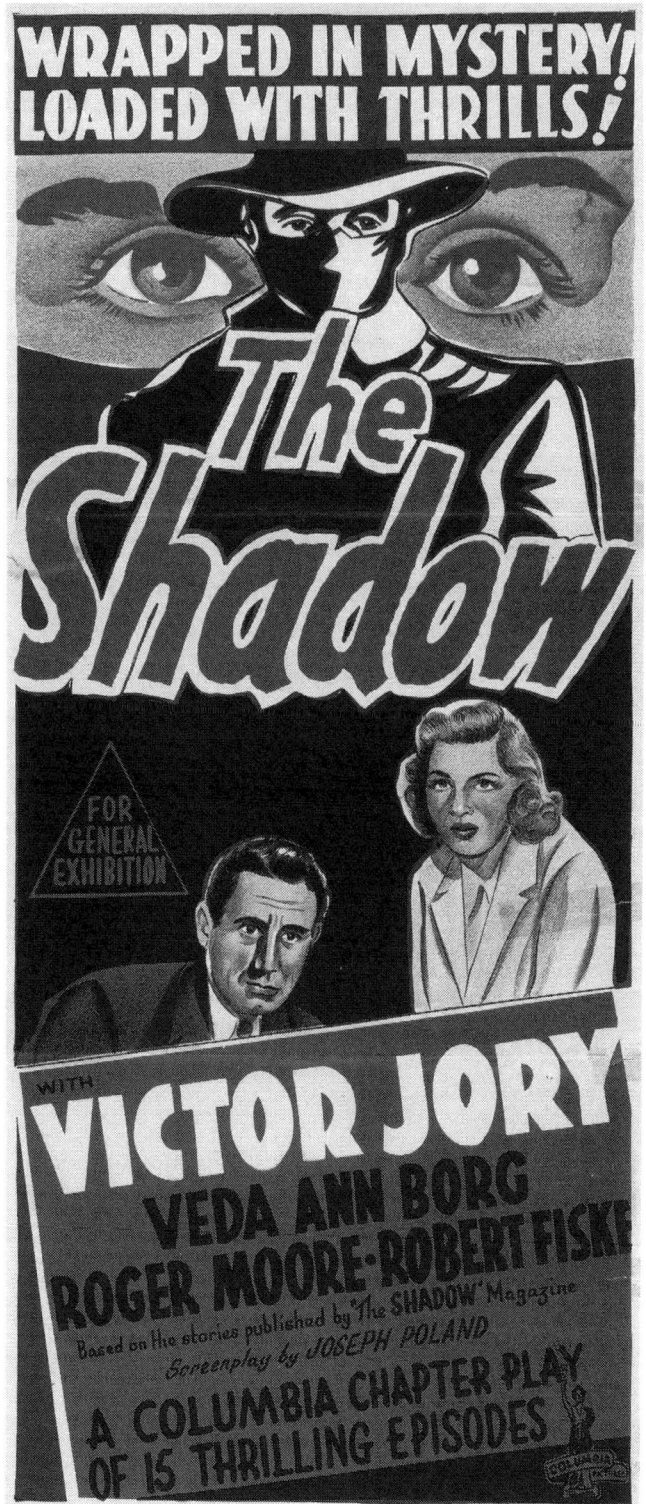

WRAPPED IN MYSTERY! LOADED WITH THRILLS!

The Shadow

FOR GENERAL EXHIBITION

WITH VICTOR JORY

VEDA ANN BORG
ROGER MOORE · ROBERT FISKE

Based on the stories published by "The SHADOW" Magazine

Screenplay by JOSEPH POLAND

A COLUMBIA CHAPTER PLAY OF 15 THRILLING EPISODES

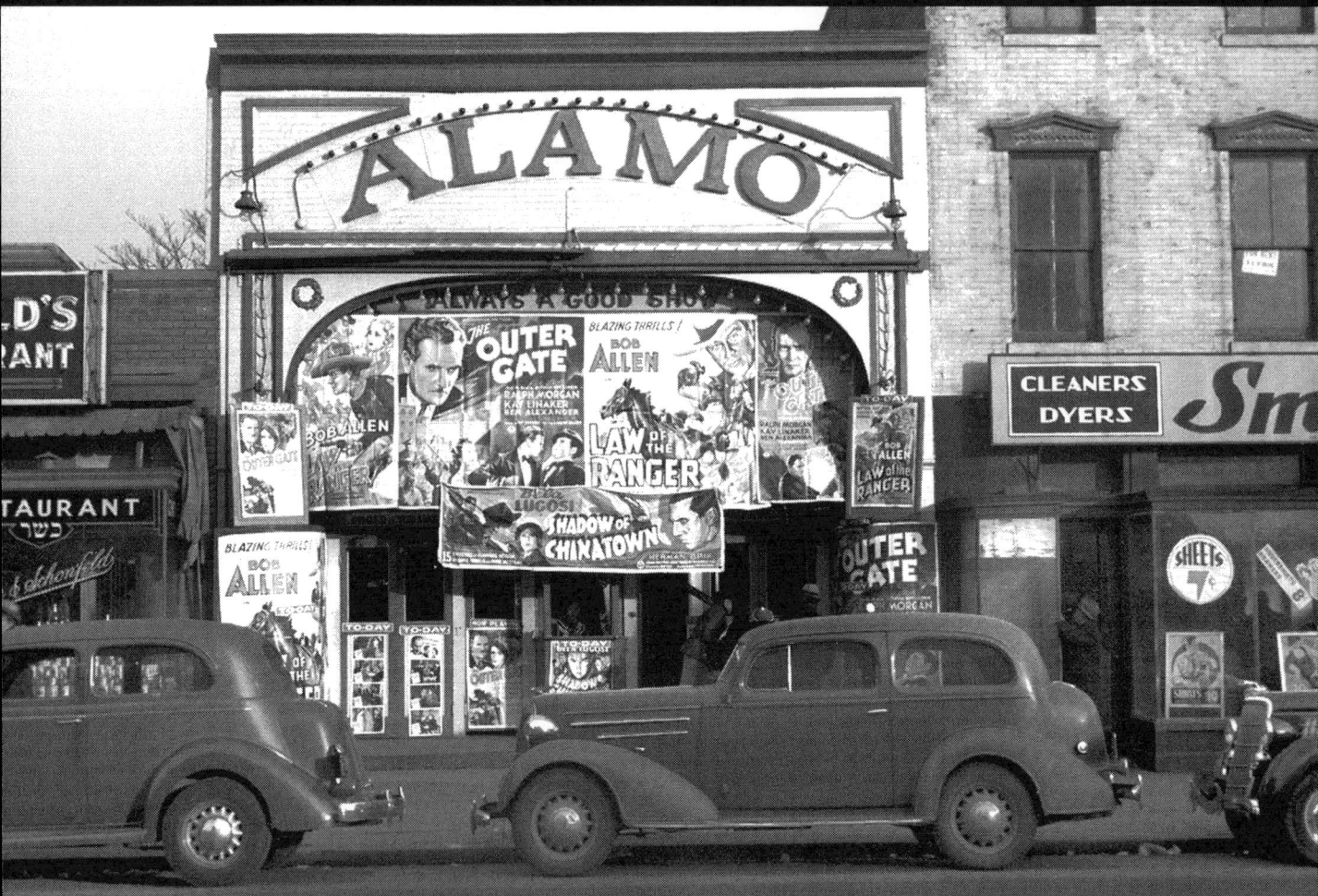

respect, it should be noted, the serial improved on *The Shadow Strikes* and *International Crime*, those dismal 1937-38 feature films starring Rod La Rocque.) However, several minor but jarring differences could be noted. Harry Vincent shuttles The Shadow to and from most of his confrontations with the Black Tiger's men. Sometimes, however, he is shown driving a taxicab and wearing a hack's cap. This suggests that the pulp Shadow's usual driver, cabbie Moe Shrevnitz, was originally included in the script, only to have his character combined with that of Vincent for cost-cutting purposes. Also, despite Street & Smith's insistence that the serial Shadow deploy his trademark automatic pistols, he uses automatics and .38-caliber revolvers interchangeably.

These inconsistencies are puzzling because

Street & Smith had specifically requested changes to the first-draft script forwarded to them by Columbia. A July 21 letter from the studio's F. L. Weber to Bill Ralston acknowledged receipt of a Street & Smith memo expressing concerns about some scenario deviations from Shadow lore. After expressing gratitude for cooperation extended to the serial's writers by Walter Gibson and *Shadow Magazine* editor John Nanovic, Weber assured Ralston that numerous minor but significant corrections would be made based on their input. "The Shadow's guns will definitely be two .45 automatics, as requested," wrote the Columbia executive. That promise went unfulfilled.

Weber also addressed the fact that Harry Vincent was occasionally seen driving a cab in usurpation of Moe Shrevnitz's function in the novels. "As regards Harry Vincent," he explained, "we are not using the character of Moe Shrevnitz. We will place a line in the first episode stating that Harry is filling in for Shrevnitz, due to his illness." Another note stated: "As regards Burbank, we are changing this character, so it will be Richards playing the role of the manservant." Both characters were regulars in the pulp yarns, but neither turned up in the Columbia chapter play, suggesting that cost-conscious Darmour had second thoughts about including them after script revisions had been made. Other changes requested by Street & Smith including changing the screenwriters' Metropolitan Club to the Cobalt Club and making Cranston an independent research scientist with his own lab, rather than an employee of Stanford Marshall, one of the industrialists targeted by the Black Tiger.

Nonetheless, The Shadow fared better in his one and only chapter play than many characters adapted from other media. Spy Smasher, for example, gained a twin brother. Blackhawk lost two of his subordinates. And Captain Marvel suffered the ignominious loss of his powers in the final chapter of *his* serial. All things considered, the Master of Darkness could have done a lot worse.

Victor Jory deserves the lion's share of credit for the serial's effectiveness. His features don't exactly match those described by Gibson as belonging to Cranston, but they come pretty close. He projects confidence and authority in the role, and it's hard not to appreciate his approximation of The Shadow's trademark laugh. "Oh, I *had* to get that right," Jory recalled in 1980. "Everybody knew that laugh, even people who didn't listen to the radio show every Sunday afternoon. It was a thing, you know, kind of like a catch phrase. 'The Shadow knows' was a popular saying. Comedians on the radio joked about it. So I practiced that chuckle until I felt I had it right. You wanted it to give the kids goose bumps; that was the idea."

James W. Horne's deliberately arch directorial style makes it difficult for today's viewers to appreciate *The Shadow*, which Columbia TriStar Home Video released on VHS cassettes in 1997. The combination of overacting, undercranking, and what film historian William K. Everson called "moments of truly lunatic comedy involving the villains" irritates serial buffs used to the more serious chapter plays of other studios. (Hardcore devotees take particular umbrage at a scene in which one of the Tiger's henchmen implores another, "Tell me the story of Red Riding Hood again. I *like* that one.") But Everson, in his introduction to Alan G. Barbour's 1970 history of serials, *Days of Thrills and Adventure*, probably got it right: "[Horne] was too good a director, too much a past master of great silent and sound comedy, not to know precisely what he was doing. Undoubtedly he reasoned that to play the scripts straight, with their stereotyped stories and meager budgets, could only result in serials spectacular inferior to the competitive ones issued by Republic and Universal. Playing them for comedy didn't make them better, but it did keep them lively, distinctive, and different."

Actually, of the ten Columbia chapter plays James Horne made for producer Larry Darmour before dying in 1942, *The Shadow* contains the fewest cringeworthy moments of campy humor. Unlike *The Green Archer* (1940) and *The Iron Claw* (1941), to name just two, the serial generally preserves its main character's dignity. It surely could have been more faithful to the source material, but *The Shadow* has a lot more going for it than the character's other big-screen incarnations: the two Rod La Rocques, the three 1946 Kane Richmonds produced by Monogram, and the awful 1959 compilation of busted Shadow TV pilots starring Richard Derr.

In his 1980 interview with me, Victor Jory stated: "I've been in a lot of good films and worked with many of the best stars, writers and directors in the business. But, you know, I'd have to say that more people know me from *The Shadow* than anything else I've done. I still get fan mail mentioning it. Here [at the Charlotte Western Film Fair] I've probably had a dozen people come up to me and ask me to do the laugh. It's the damnedest thing."

The Shadow was followed by three more 1940 Columbia serials adapted from properties created for other media: *Terry and the Pirates* (based on Milton Caniff's popular comic strip), *Deadwood Dick* (updating a venerable character of late-19th century dime novels), and *The Green Archer* (from Edgar Wallace's celebrated mystery novel, previously turned into a wildly successful serial by Pathé in 1925). If one is to believe exhibitor reports published in the trade journal Motion Picture Herald, the Shadow serial was the most popular of the quartet. But apparently not so much as to induce Columbia to produce a sequel, especially since the contract with Street & Smith called for a bump in the licensing fee to $8500 should the studio want to revisit the character.

It still remains to be seen whether Hollywood will ever produce a Shadow movie that does full justice to the pulp-magazine version of the character as developed by Walter B. Gibson so long ago. For several years now it's been rumored that another feature film was being developed. Perhaps there's a future director out there, reading Anthony Tollin's Sanctum Books reprints and envisioning a faithful Shadow screen story as I write these words. *BT*

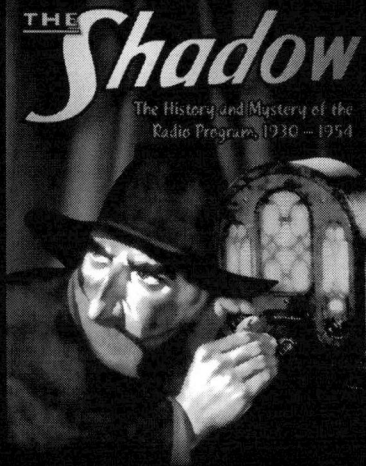

The Green Lama

by Martin Grams, Jr.

In 1936, newly married writer Kendell Foster Crossen—eager to secure a full-time salaried position during those mid-Depression years—joined the Frank A. Munsey Company and became an assistant editor on *Detective Fiction Weekly*. After several years he came to the realization that Munsey's regular pulp writers were making a lot more money than he was. Crossen gambled that he could do as well and quit in 1939 to freelance full time.

Not surprisingly, Crossen specialized in detective yarns and made most of his sales to the Munsey group. The next year he was offered an opportunity craved by many writers in the field: the chance to write regular novel-length stories about a character of his own devising.

"The Green Lama came into existence in a sort of off-hand manner," Crossen told pop-culture historian Ron Goulart in 1969. "*Double Detective* [a Munsey magazine that had been around for nearly three years without ever meeting the expectations for it] wasn't doing too well and they wanted to fresh it up. I had nothing to do with editing it but was called in on conferences with [editorial director A. J.] Gibney and Paul Johnson, who was the editor, about what could be done. It was finally decided to do something to compete with The Shadow and I was asked to draw up an outline for such a character. The result was the Green Lama (first called the Gray Lama but changed for reasons of color on the cover) and I was also asked to write it. I did 18 [*Editor's Note: actually, 14*] Green Lama novels under the name of Richard Foster. They ran to about 40,000 words each."

The Green Lama was actually wealthy playboy Jethro Dumont. According to the standard

Ken Crossen during his pulp-writing days.

description repeated—with minor variations—from issue to issue, he "had fallen heir to a fortune estimated at ten million dollars while still at Harvard. It was during his college days that he first became interested in the Oriental religions. Shortly after his graduation he went to Tibet and studied for several years, later becoming a fully ordained priest in the Lamaist sect of Buddhism. He then returned to America and took up residence on Park Avenue."

What would have attracted such a spiritual person to the apprehension of criminals is a question the stories never satisfactorily answered. While on the mean streets in character, Dumont wore a green hood and robe. While

pursuing leads he often impersonated one Doctor Pali, a Buddhist cleric who wore a dark green suit, light green shirt, and similarly shaded collar. As the Green Lama he carried no weapon save a dark red *kara* (scarf), which was draped around his neck when not in use. He was given to chanting the ritual mantra, "Om mani padme hum," and stuck terror in the hearts of evildoers for reasons never made apparent.

The Green Lama novels extended the life of *Double Detective* by several years, even after Popular Publications bought the Munsey chain in 1943. Crossen later wrote comic-book stories featuring the character in addition to other detective yarns for pulps and hardcovers. He published under several pseudonyms, the best known being M. E. Chaber. Eventually he drifted into dramatic radio as well, writing scripts for some of the top crime and mystery shows. One of them was *The Saint*.

Dubbed "the Robin Hood of modern crime," the polished, urbane Simon Templar, a.k.a. The Saint, was a devil-may-care, swashbuckling do-gooder. At various times and in various mediums—he appeared in books, pulps, movies, and comic strips—Templar worked on both sides of the law. Primarily an adventurer, he occasionally functioned as a private eye. The Saint, created by Leslie Charteris, maintained a healthy run on radio from 1945 to 1951. The program's scripts didn't always accurately reflect the character that appeared in the Charteris novels, but they were accepted by radio audiences craving a good mystery, and they found favor with the program's sponsors: Bromo-Seltzer, Campbell Soups, Ford, and Pepsodent. The success of *The Saint* can be attributed to scriptwriters Michael Cramoy, Louis Vittes, and Ken Crossen.

In early 1948, Crossen wrote a radio script for *The Saint* titled "Babies for Sale." Simon Templar's girlfriend, Patricia Holm, is doing volunteer social work when she meets Horace J. Atwood and philanthropist Gordon Phillips, who work at the Sanctuary Foundling Home, a free

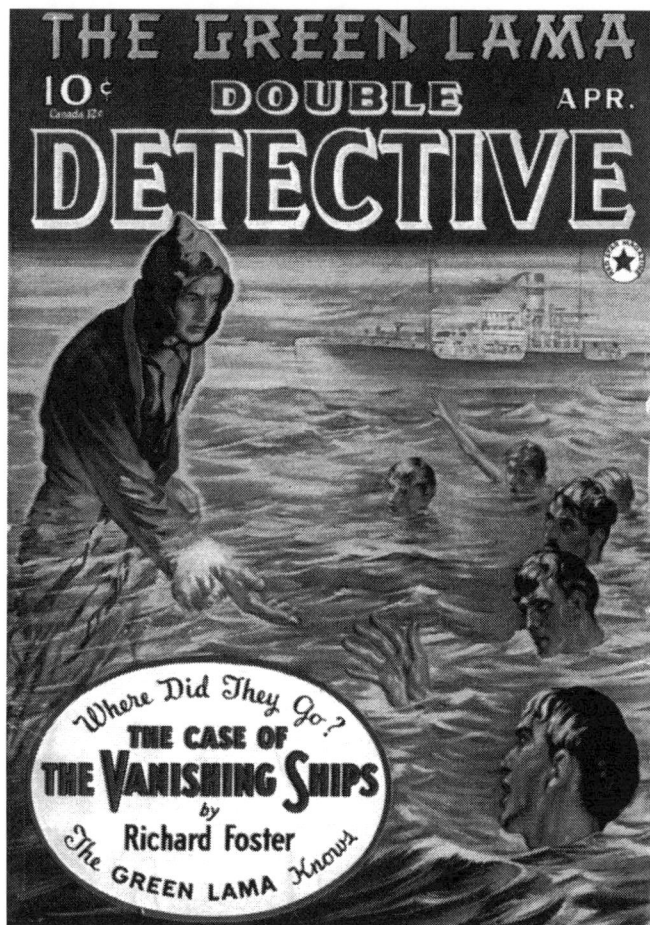

maternity hospital for indigent women. The "maternity hospital," however, is running a three-fold racket. After telling the mothers their newborns have died, the hospital illegally puts the babies up for adoption, demanding large "donations" in addition to a thousand-dollar fee imposed on the adoptive parents. Denton, an ex-con working in cahoots with the hospital executives, then blackmails the adoptive parents after convincing them that he is the baby's real father. After tricking a confession out of Denton, Templar approaches the guilty parties, including Atwood, whereupon the police overhear the details of the plot and arrest the culprits.

The above synopsis, based on a radio script found in the Kendell F. Crossen collection at the Howard Gotlieb Archival Research Center at

Less than ten percent of all radio broadcasts before 1960 are known to exist in recorded form. More than half of *The Green Lama* radio broadcasts from 1949 are among the missing.

Boston University, is about all we know of this particular episode of *The Saint*—except that the unproduced script was loosely based on the Green Lama adventure of the same title, originally published in the June 1940 issue of *Double Detective* (and reprinted in Volume One of The Green Lama pulp-reprint trilogy published by Altus Press). Both stories took place in Hollywood, California. Instead of a maternity hospital, the original pulp story involved a home for orphaned children.

It is believed that Crossen wrote the script circa February or March of 1948 but never actually made the sale. The subject matter might have been considered taboo to producer James Saphier, and a few loose ends (such as why Atwood would even bother to ask Templar to investigate) no doubt further hindered the story from making the grade.

It has become a commonplace of radio scholarship that less than ten percent of all radio broadcasts before 1960 are known to exist in recorded form. And it is regrettable that more than half of *The Green Lama* radio broadcasts from 1949 are among the missing. Naturally, Crossen's involvement with the radio program did not include paying for transcription discs to be recorded. He was focused on story structure and plot proposals.

Very little is known about Ken Crossen's career writing scripts for radio mysteries. Only recently have excavations of Library of Congress records revealed some of his earliest known efforts, mainly as a contributor for *The Molle Mystery Theatre*, which premiered over NBC on September 7, 1943, featuring dramatizations of classic and current mystery stories. The novels, short sto-

ries, and original mysteries were introduced by a mysterious narrator named Geoffrey Barnes, a distinguished criminologist played by actor Roc Rogers. The stories of Cornell Woolrich, Craig Rice, Edgar Wallace, and many other creators of modern detective fiction were adapted for the program by scriptwriters Jay Bennett, Charles Tazewell, and Everett George Opie.

Crossen's first assignment for *The Molle Mystery Theatre* was an adaptation of Raymond Chandler's *Lady in the Lake*, broadcast on the evening of December 14, 1943. An admirer of Chandler's writing, Crossen happily adapted several of the *Black Mask* graduate's stories, including *Farewell My Lovely* (February 29, 1944), *Goldfish* (July 18, 1944) and *Murder in City Hall*, a.k.a. *Spanish Blood* (September 14, 1944). While the exact number of Crossen's radio scripts remain unknown, four others have been verified. Dwight V. Babcock's *Homicide for Hannah* (December 28, 1943), Michael Venning's *Murder Through the Looking Glass* (September 5, 1944), and Jonathan Pierce's *A Crime to Fit the Punishment* (December 5, 1944), the last co-scripted with H. L. Gold. For the broadcast of June 20, 1944, Crossen chose to adapt the Richard Powell novel *Death Talks Out of Turn*, cleverly designed to remind radio listeners that "loose lips sink ships." The story involved a spy ring in contact with an enemy sub offshore and plotting to blow up an Allied ship as it prepares to set sail with its load

Crossen continued writing scripts for radio mysteries, including one for *The Adventures of Ellery Queen*. In "Nikki Porter, Killer" (March 5, 1947), Ellery comes to the rescue when his secretary/girlfriend Nikki, suffering amnesia, steps off a train just as the loot from a bank robbery disappears from her compartment and a man is found murdered. While the majority of the Ellery Queen radio broadcasts from 1947 and 1948 exist on transcription disc, the March 5 broadcast does not. In 1954 and 1955, the Ellery Queen radio program aired on Australian airwaves, courtesy of Grace Gibson Radio Productions. Purchasing scripts from the U.S., Gibson's staff at the Australian Record Company performed their own renditions, with minor but essential alterations such as changing New York City to Sydney. The only extant copy of the Crossen-scripted episode in collector hands is in the form of the Australian counterpart.

Crossen did succeed in selling one script to *The Saint:* "With No Tomorrow," broadcast on May 19, 1948. It tells the tale of Warner Wilson, an executive of the exporting firm of Wilson and Lynn, who believes he is the victim of a monstrous plot. With the removals of his birth certificate at the Bureau of Vital Statistics and his records at the Bureau of Motor Vehicles, it seems as if his entire life is being erased. Fearing for his sanity, the executive turns to Simon Templar for help. The Saint's investigation of the murder of Wilson's business partner, Jerome Lane, finally unmasks the guilty culprit, Stephen Hurley, a young politician with ambitions for both Wilson's wife and the money she would inherit upon her husband's death. Hurley devised an elaborate scheme to drive Wilson crazy and cause the two business partners to have a deadly falling-out. Templar's intervention proves without a shred of doubt that Hurley committed the crimes. Regrettably, no recording of this drama is known to exist.

Among the most prestigious radio programs at that time was *Suspense,* broadcast over CBS, pro-

> ## "Ken might say otherwise but it was I who convinced CBS to broadcast the program."
> — producer/director Norman MacDonnell

duced on a large budget (courtesy of the Auto-Lite Company), and featuring a Hollywood star every week. Soon after Anton M. Leader took over the producing/directing chores for *Suspense* in early 1948, Crossen learned that he purchased scripts from the open market (before the days of studio policy that declared reviewing unsolicited scripts was a legal liability). The former pulp writer approached Leader with a total of three radio scripts, all adaptations of classic mysteries: "The Hands of Mr. Ottermole" (December 2, 1948), John Collier's "De Mortuis" (February 10, 1949), and "Murder Through the Looking Glass" (March 17, 1949). The third and final broadcast was loosely rewritten from his former *Molle Mystery* script.

It was during his CBS tenure that Crossen was introduced to producer/director Norman MacDonnell. MacDonnell had purchased the radio rights to Graham Greene's 1939 novel, *Confidential Agent*—which, like many Greene properties, proved difficult to adapt for broadcast. Crossen agreed to take on the task and succeeded. The story involved a chivalrous agent who starts out as a hunted man and becomes the hunter, a peaceful man who turns at bay, and a man who learned to love justice by suffering injustice. It was recorded on March 30, 1949 and broadcast three days later.

MacDonnell and Crossen struck up a friendship. "Ken was very ambitious and high strung," recalled MacDonnell in a 1971 interview. "Always nervous and looking over his shoulder. . . . He was a smooth pitchman who knew the right words to say when he wanted something. Ken submitted a radio script adapted from his Green Lama creation. I believe this was for *Escape.* After I looked over it, I discouraged him, briefly, by asking for a revision to fit the mold of a weekly sustainer. Establish the plot, format, recurring

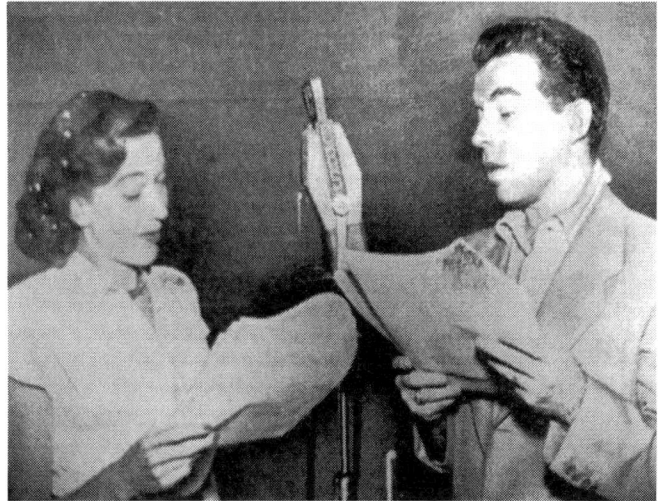

characters, and so forth. . . . Ken might say otherwise but it was I who convinced CBS to broadcast the program."

Knowing that *Broadway Is My Beat* was going off the air for the summer, MacDonnell pitched the Green Lama show to CBS executives for that same time slot. Ken Crossen agreed to write the radio scripts but MacDonnell, fearing the former pulpster did not have enough experience to complete a full 30-page script every week, assigned William Froug to co-write. Froug was a newcomer to the field, having already helped create the *Rocky Jordan* radio program, and served as a mentor to Crossen.

There has been some speculation that Crossen only created the plots and Froug wrote the actual scripts. This appears to be a myth because further review of the radio scripts reveals many Crossen trademarks and influences. They include not one but two direct references to Philip Marlowe and one reference to Raymond Chandler.

Taking a page from the *Shadow* radio program, the Green Lama's audio adventures varied considerably from the pulp stories. In the pulps, Jethro Dumont had several agents who helped gather information used to deduce criminal motives and methods. One of these agents was a mysterious woman called "Magga," whose real identity was never revealed. On radio, Dumont traversed the globe accompanied by a Tibetan manservant, Tulku (played by Ben Wright), who was Dumont's only agent in the combat against crime.

The early episodes injected comic relief in the form of cab drivers who offered Dumont their assistance for small fees. As in the pulps, the Green Lama applied supernatural powers to fight evil wherever he encountered it. The show's introduction identified him as waging a "single-handed fight against injustice and crime." (Single-handed because radio's Lama eschewed the Dr. Pali alias.) The pulp efforts to educate readers about the Buddhist faith were discarded, as was Dumont's use of "radioactive salt" to enhance his powers.

In the pulps, Jethro Dumont traveled across the globe as lecturer to spread basic Buddhist doctrines. He did so on two particular radio programs, but his exact profession, or how he financed his activities, was never fully revealed. The pulps explained how, having inherited ten million dollars from his father, Dumont was able to devote his time to ridding the world of evil. Radio listeners unfamiliar with the pulps could only infer that he was independently wealthy and had no need to work. The Green Lama's indifference to money was evident when, in one episode, a man named Harrison Bigelow attempted to hire Dumont for his services:

DUMONT: Mr. Bigelow, you mentioned hiring me. If you know anything about me, you must know I'm not for hire.

BIGELOW: Nonsense. Every man is for hire—it's only a question of finding his price. I was thinking about ten thousand dollars for you.

DUMONT: I said I'm not for hire.

BIGELOW: (HARD) Fifteen thousand dollars.

DUMONT: You know, you're beginning to interest me, Mr. Bigelow. Is there anything that you think you can't buy?

BIGELOW: I'll make it twenty thousand dollars, Mr. Dumont, but not a cent more.

TULKU: It is written that when money talks it is nearly always with a raised voice.

DUMONT: You are so right, Tulku. . . . Mr. Bigelow, I'll break an old habit and let you hire me for twenty thousand dollars—on two conditions.

BIGELOW: What are they?

DUMONT: First, make the check payable to the Cancer Fund. I'll tell you the second condition after I have the check.

BIGELOW: All right.

SOUND: WRITING OF CHECK.

JESSICA: Ouch! Jethro—you're just costing me half of my next week's allowance.

DUMONT: How is that?

JESSICA: I bet Harrison that he couldn't hire you.

DUMONT: Then perhaps this will teach you not to gamble, Mrs. Bigelow.

JESSICA: Not at all, Jethro. I bet him the other half of my allowance that you'd never pick up the paintings.

SOUND: TEARING CHECK OUT OF BOOK

BIGELOW: There you are, Mr. Dumont. Now, what is the second condition?

DUMONT: That you tell me the truth.

BIGELOW: What? You mean to say—

DUMONT: (INTERRUPTING)—that you're lying?

Yes. You may want to present the paintings to the university all right, but that's not why you're willing to pay me twenty thousand dollars to pick them up! I want the truth—or we can just forget the whole thing.

BIGELOW: But you've already accepted the check.

DUMONT: I've accepted your check as a donation to a worthy cause. I haven't accepted your employment.

JESSICA: (LAUGHS) You know, Jethro—you interest me more and more. Harrison, I think he has you on the hook. You'd better tell him the truth.

The radio scripts were written with the assumption that listeners had not read the pulp magazines. The Green Lama was described in a single paragraph at the beginning of each episode:

And now we bring you another exciting adventure taken directly from the files of Jethro Dumont—the wealthy young American who, after ten years in Tibet, returned as the Green Lama to amaze the world with his curious and secret powers in his single-handed fight against crime!

When pressed for details, Dumont's Tulku, explained further:

Many have wondered why Jethro Dumont is called the Green Lama. Jethro Dumont is a lama because of his great wisdom and powers of concentration, and the Green Lama because green is one of the six sacred colors and is the symbol of justice.

The opening "billboard" (expository narration) was revised beginning with episode eight:

From the mystery of the Far East—from the mountain peaks of a Shangri-la—from Tibet—

come the exciting adventures of Jethro Dumont. Jethro Dumont, the wealthy young American who, after ten years in Tibet, returned as the Green Lama to carry on a single-handed fight against injustice and crime. It is the wisdom and power of concentration, enabling the Green Lama to do things impossible for ordinary men, which has made him the nemesis of the underworld!

Exactly what those powers were, other than receiving visions after closing his eyes and clearing his thoughts, probably remained unknown to listeners. Physical combat sometimes included a chant beforehand, but action was depicted in the same manner as private eyes who wrestled a gun out of a thug's hand.

None of the radio broadcasts adapted specific Green Lama stories, but they borrowed elements and locales from Crossen's novels. Eleven episodes were produced at the CBS studios in

Los Angeles. Supposedly, an audition recording was produced on the afternoon of May 17, 1949. While there appear to be two different recordings of "The Man Who Never Existed" in circulation (with an eight-minute difference in length, and different dialogue and music cues), nothing has been found to verify the date May 17. A few sources report June 2 as the recording date.

On June 8, *Variety* reviewed the premiere broadcast and referred to *The Green Lama* as "satisfactory hot-weather stuff, with exotic atmosphere added as extra whodunit flavor. Format follows the usual air crime mystery motif, but judged by Sunday's premiere, interest is sustained by good writing, acting, and situation. Colloquial dialog, a slew of false clues, and good performances helped put the program over. Paul Frees, as the Green Lama, is convincing, and support is good."

Two of radio's busiest actors, both with readily identifiable voices, appeared in the leads. The title character was played by talented Paul Frees, future voice of the Pillsbury Doughboy and *Rocky & Bullwinkle*'s dastardly Boris Badenov, as well as ghost host of Disneyland's Haunted Mansion, occasional movie bit-player, and the narrator of countless coming-attractions trailers. Ben Wright, who sported an authentic British accent (and acted in several West End stage productions in England before the war), played the role of Tulku similar to that of Hey Boy on radio's *Have Gun—Will Travel* nine years later. Wright also doubled as a British Captain and an Inspector for two broadcasts. Actor Herb Vigran played the recurring role of New York police sergeant Weylan, but his appearances were limited to three episodes because not all the adventures took place in New York City. The supporting cast included Georgia Ellis, Parley Baer, Howard McNear, John Dehner, and William Conrad. Larry Thor was the announcer.

The first eight episodes featured continuity that carried over with a mention of the previous week's adventure. If Tulku was shot and injured

Tulku discussing a newspaper article that intrigued them, a mystery they intended to file away as "The Adventure of . . . ," offering a tease of next week's adventure for the benefit of listeners. The next week, however, found them experiencing or witnessing the deed described in last week's newspapers! Could the radio audience have been so observant as to notice this break in continuity? The scriptwriters apparently did. This device of teasing the audience about next week's drama was reduced to a passing mention (instead of the characters' reading about it in the newspaper) and dropped altogether in the last two broadcasts.

The Green Lama offered some offbeat settings and situations. In "The Million Dollar Chopsticks," Jethro and Tulku arrive in Hong Kong to solve a murder and a theft. In "The Last Dinosaur," a woman is found murdered by the swimming pool at a Hollywood cocktail party, and evidence suggests a baby dinosaur was the culprit. "The Last Dinosaur," which exists in recorded form,

in one broadcast, a mention that he was recovering was made at the beginning of the next. In the beginning of episode seven, the servant makes mention of enjoying the teas of France, locale of the last week's adventure. This system of maintaining continuity was discontinued with Episode Nine. but was applied in a number of the pulp novels, additional evidence that Crossen had a larger hand in the development of the scripts than initially conceived.

Early episodes concluded with Jethro and also features an inside joke: famed Hollywood columnist George Fisher plays himself at the party. In "The Adventure of the Perfect Prisoner," a talented sculptor named Frank Cobb is knifed to death just as he is about to released from a "model prison" after securing a pardon. When Dumont investigates, he becomes embroiled in a prison riot and is confronted by hundreds of inmates attempting to escape. Other adventures took Jethro and Tulku to Cairo ("The Man Who Stole a Pyramid"), Paris ("The Return of Madame

Pompadour"), and Havana ("The Case of the Dangerous Dog").

Many radio heroes spent time looking over their shoulders for baddies who lurked in dark alleys. Criminal psychologists, international couriers, and U. S. Intelligence agents were heard at least three times every night on the major networks—making *The Green Lama* just another crime program, with little to distinguish it from the competition.

In an epilogue to one episode, the Green Lama painstakingly expounded on each clue, proving he had outsmarted the criminals. But the details were so refined that most auditors would have considered them assumptions, not facts. *The Adventures of Ellery Queen* was one program that gave audiences a fair chance to solve the mystery themselves. On *The Green Lama*, however, no listener could have "assumed" the facts Dumont revealed to the authorities at the conclusion of each mystery. Crossen obviously knew that his hero had to be smarter than the police, but he managed to avoid typecasting cops as dim-witted. Agitated, yes. Keystone Kops, no. Not that it mattered. The moral of every story, made crystal-clear to the audience, was still: "Crime does not pay."

Unlike many of its radio competitors, *The Green Lama* never featured a love interest, such as a flirtatious secretary. However, in almost every episode a beautiful woman—married or single—expressed her attraction to the Green Lama. This was never more evident than in the previously excerpted "Tapestry in Purple," when married Jessica Bigelow proposed taking Dumont back home for a spell. True to form, he rejected her advances.

Although Jethro Dumont never drank liquor like Sam Spade, Dashiell Hammett's *The Maltese Falcon* clearly inspired the format of the *Green Lama* radio program. In half the cases, criminals double-crossed and killed their partners-in-crime. Others offered Dumont a fee ten times larger than the value of the stolen property he was hired to recover. His clients generally wanted

to avoid the police, for reasons that were soon made obvious.

The Green Lama was in a class of his own, compared with other detectives on the airwaves. But then, every private detective on radio was distinguished in some way. In *The Private Files of Matthew Bell* (1952), a police surgeon drew upon his medical skills to solve crimes. The title character of *Yours Truly, Johnny Dollar* (1949–1962) was a private insurance investigator with an expense account which he would itemize for his clients, thus explaining how he went about investigating the weekly mystery. *I Deal in Crime* (1946–1948) found ex-seaman Ross Dolan, suddenly relieved of nautical duty, returning to his old profession of Los Angeles-based private eye. In *Mystery Is My Hobby* (1945–1946), Barton Drake, a mystery writer doubled as a police detective. *Dear Margie, It's Murder* (1953) had as its gimmick an American vet studying in England under the G. I. Bill while finding time to assist a Scotland Yard inspector. (The show's title referred to letters Drake wrote to his girlfriend back home, regaling her with accounts of his sleuthing experiences.)

Jethro Dumont and Tulku often exchanged proverbs that must have baffled the average radio listener. "It is written that silence is the only true friend of discretion" and "It is written that the unspoken word watches over the hidden action" are two such examples. The scriptwriters went overboard with proverbs during the earliest broadcasts, but eventually cut them down to two or three per broadcast. Radio listeners unfamiliar with the pulp stories on which the series was based might have considered *The Green Lama* a bland imitation of *Charlie Chan*.

By 1949, radio audiences were overwhelmed with more private detectives than they could keep track of. Almost all were brash, abrasive gumshoes who brushed up against beautiful women, resentful and impatient police inspectors, and an assortment of bookies, touts, and stool pigeons—many of them silenced by fatal bullets before revealing important clues. More than one dead body (and usually three, as a general rule) fell within the first 20 minutes of any given program. *The Green Lama* was no exception to this pattern.

If anything, *The Green Lama* fell into the *Sam Spade* clutch. *The Adventures of Sam Spade* premiered in the summer of 1946 and broke new ground as a weekly private-eye show. Spade stole money from a dead man's wallet, bedded married women, and drank booze while dictating his capers to his secretary. Within two years, detective programs ran rampant on all the major networks, but none of them pushed the borders of decency as commonly as pulp magazines, where censorship was lax. When the original writers of the *Sam Spade* program departed for greener pastures, the new scripters were unable to maintain the sharp edge that made the program so venerated. As a result, the series ultimately fell back on the same tropes used by its competition, which tried so hard to imitate Spade. This has since become known as the "*Sam Spade* clutch," and it wasn't until two days before the premiere of *The Green Lama* on CBS that Jack Webb's new NBC program, *Dragnet*, broke new ground, elevating the "police procedural" format and making the other detective programs seem weak by comparison.

This was no fault of *The Green Lama*. In the radio industry, timing was everything and sensational sponsor contracts dictated the longevity of a program. Without a sponsor, and with Norman MacDonnell's departure, *The Green Lama* was bound to fail. Nonetheless, CBS allowed the program to air anyway, sustained by the hope that a potential sponsor would sign a contract. Part of the problem may have been the growing concern about blood-'n'-thunder programs, which concerned parents were campaigning against. Radio thrillers (and comic books) were considered bad influences on young children, who would mimic the cops-and-robbers lingo. According to a CBS inter-office memo dated July 15, 1949, an unnamed insurance company in New York expressed interest, in sponsoring *The Green Lama* as long as the program aired at a later time slot to avoid "apprehensive parents and their lettering."

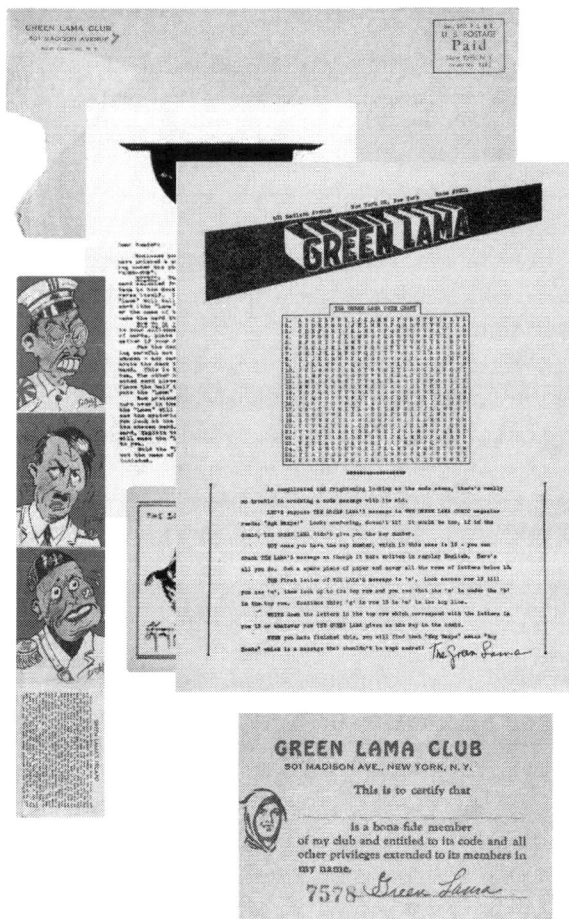

For the final two broadcasts of the series, Gene Levitt and Bob Mitchell were brought in to co-write the scripts under the supervision of Ken Crossen, who still provided the plots but nothing more. This ultimately meant bewildering changes in character for Jethro Dumont. He displayed a short fuse but was also depicted as lighthearted, discarding the solemn persona radio listeners were used to.

Today, enthusiasts of Old-Time Radio regard this short-run program as a mere curiosity. Recent articles in club newsletters describe the series as "a sleeper" and "a rather easygoing adventure." Anyone reading the radio scripts would consider the series below par. However, under the capable direction of Norman MacDonnell (who would later bring *Gunsmoke* to CBS airwaves), the series offered above-average production values.

The Green Lama never offered premiums to listeners, and neither the pulps nor comic books were still being produced in 1949—so there was no opportunity for the cross-promotion that might have increased consumer awareness of the character. According to the October 29, 1949, issue of *Television-Billboard Magazine,* CBS still retained the broadcasting option for *The Green Lama,* among other radio programs, and the show was considered for television adaptation. But *The Green Lama* never made it to TV, so the last broadcast of August 20, 1949, contained the character's final utterance of his chant of justice.

EPISODE LIST

Episode #1: "The Man Who Never Existed"
Original Broadcast Date: Sunday, June 5, 1949.
Plot: Soon after Jethro Dumont arrives in New York, his good friend Professor Hendrix is found murdered. The only clue is the recent robbery at the Museum of Primitive Art. One of Professor Hendrix's discoveries, a Kulkulcan, was stolen from the Mayan exhibit. Discovering that Hendrix himself stole the piece and mailed it back to the excavation site in Mexico, Dumont and his faithful servant, Tulku, book tickets to fly south. In Mexico, Dumont meets Marta Hendrix, the professor's daughter, and discovers the stolen Kulkulcan was a fake. Philmore Merton, director of the museum, flies to Mexico in the hopes of recovering the stolen artifact before anyone discovers (as Professor Hendrix did) that he was selling the original pieces and replacing them with fakes. Merton is too late, however, because Dumont already solved the case and found the proof. Merton is apprehended and flown back to New York to face a charge of murder.

Episode #2: "The Man Who Stole a Pyramid"
Original Broadcast Date: Sunday, June 12, 1949.
Plot: The Green Lama, attending the reception of the grand opening of the newly excavated Mastaba Pyramid of King Kbebe, is shocked to discover the massive stone structure has completely vanished outside city limits of Cairo, Egypt. The local authorities, as well as Jethro Dumont, are baffled. The prime suspect is Count Nikolai Sumotkin, a pyramidologist who believes the future can be told according to the physical measurements of the pyramids, and who predicted the disappearance the night before. As Jethro wanders Egypt investigating the details of the case, Hussein el-Had, chairman of the Pyramid commission, is stabbed to death. Another attempt on Jethro's life leads to a clue that ultimately solves the mystery. Mr. Cartwright, owner of an American oil well, was operating an illegal enterprise. Cartwright tapped the main oil pipeline and ran a spur to the pyramid. Then he stored oil in the chambers below and from this reserve he sold oil that was supposed to come from his well. If the pyramid were opened, his scheme would fail. All he did was dynamite the foundations so that the pyramid fell down into the first chamber and the sandstorm covered the hole with sand. The Green Lama apprehends the guilty party and turns him over to the police.

Episode #3: "The Girl with No Name"
Original Broadcast Date: Sunday, June 19, 1949.
Plot: The Green Lama and Tulku answer a plea from Susan Carter, who fears her uncle, an engineer, may be involved in a recent rash of subway booth robberies. When a subway train carrying the day's payload from the change booths suddenly vanishes almost before their eyes, Jethro Dumont and Tulku investigate. They soon discover an unfinished and deserted tunnel where the train secretly vanished, masked by dirty beaverboard that looks the same color as rock, fooling investigators. After rescuing Susan's uncle, the Green Lama witnesses the murder of George

Carter, and realizing dead men tell no tales, pieces the clues together. Leslie Leeds, who claimed to have witnessed the attempted murder of Susan Carter, was working hand-in-hand with Harry Betes, an employee at the change booth, and hired a gang of thugs to steal the payroll. Exposed, the crooks are taken into custody by Sgt. Weylan.

Episode #4: "The Million Dollar Chopsticks"
Original Broadcast Date: Sunday, June 26, 1949.
Plot: In Hong Kong, a city of Oriental charm and beauty, there was a murder involving a pair of chopsticks said to be worth one million dollars. The Green Lama faced death and violence in order to help a friend, Rita Randolph, discover how her business partner, Toby Holbrook, cheated her out of the money she invested. When

Holbrook staggers into Rita's hotel apartment with a knife in his back, the Green Lama investigates to uncover the facts: the business venture was masking a smuggling operation involving small emeralds looted from Peking. The chopsticks are hollow and the emeralds were placed inside. Howard Stacey, would-be playboy, partnered with Holbrook. When Rita claimed a pair of chopsticks, unaware of what was inside them, the guilty culprits attempted to retrieve them and Stacey tried to eliminate his business partner. Confronting the Green Lama, Stacey falls overboard and, unable to swim, drowns.

Episode #5: "The Last Dinosaur"
Original Broadcast Date: Sunday, July 3, 1949.
Plot: The LaBrea Tar Pits in Hollywood are famous for having preserved the fossils of prehistoric animals, and it is rumored all over the glamour city that a live dinosaur came out of the pits and is loose in Hollywood. A publicity stunt gone bad for Herman K. Herman's latest picture, *The Last Dinosaur,* or a masquerade for murder? The discovery of the body of Gloria Spear at Herman's latest Hollywood party suggests a dinosaur was the culprit. The Green Lama suspects otherwise. Further investigation leads to Triumph Pictures and the murder of the film's producer, Herman K. Herman. After confronting a raging dinosaur on the lot, the Green Lama throws himself against one of its legs so it will go off balance and fall. The murderer was Mary Carter, who controlled the mechanical dinosaur used for the motion picture. In love with Herman and jealous of Gloria's engagement to him, she had faked the dinosaur footprints by the swimming pool where Gloria's body was found.

Episode #6: "The Return of Madame Pompadour"
Original Broadcast Date: Saturday, July 16, 1949.
Plot: The Tusconi Wax Museum in France unveils the new likeness of Jeanne Antoinette Poisson le Normant d'Etioles, also known as the Marquise de Pompadour. When Lilly Jardin, the model for

the wax figure, is stabbed to death, Jethro Dumont suspects a connection with the theft of the Pompadour necklace. Sam Pulowski, an American formerly employed by the National Library, was responsible for the theft. It isn't until a slip of the lip that Dumont figures out how Pulowski accomplished the feat. He hid the necklace around the statue's neck until the heat was off, but after learning that the statue was not good enough and a replacement was needed, Pulowski panicked and began killing the people responsible for issuing the replacement. This meant killing the model, Lilly, as well.

Episode #7: "Tapestry in Purple"
Original Broadcast Date: Saturday, July 23, 1949.
Plot: Harrison Bigelow hires Jethro Dumont to retrieve a delivery of ten valuable Tibetan paint-ings of Azmu Sah'ai that are scheduled for arrival at the local airport. Dumont accepts the job, only to discover two crooks, René Sebastian and Sidney, are after the same goods. When the paintings fail to arrive at the airport and Dahli Han from Tibet claims they were stolen property, Dumont investigates the details of the case. When the shipping clerk at the airport is shot dead and Harrison Bigelow is murdered in his office, Dumont leads the police to the Bigelow home where he reveals the facts. Jessica Bigelow, widow, partnered with René and Sidney to retrieve a valuable purple tapestry known as the Seventh Return of Buddha, hidden in the frame of one of the paintings. The guilty parties are apprehended and the tapestry is handed over to Dahli Han, who will oversee its return to the rightful owners.

Episode #8: "The Worthless Diamond"
Original Broadcast Date: Saturday, July 30, 1949.
Plot: Jethro Dumont flies down to Vallpris, South Africa, to assist Hans Judkin with a problem. It seems diamonds discovered in a new mine are not only genuine, but have created chaos, disorder, and riots because money-hungry men have flocked into town to purchase land and mine it for valuable gems. Before he can reveal his suspicions, Judkin is shot dead in the street. Louise Lanier, owner of the Diamond Palace, a gambling hall, seems to be one of the few to profit from the new strangers' arrival in town, but she isn't the only suspect. Damos, her servant, threatened Dumont's life. When Damos is stabbed to death in the gambling hall, Dumont asks Eddie, the barkeep, to escort him to Lanier's private diamond mine. That's where the solution is revealed: Vino Simmons has been mining her private real estate and then claimed a diamond discovery elsewhere to keep the new arrivals from discovering the real source. Sir Hubert, the local real estate agent, profited from half of the diamonds and the sale of real estate. Dumont apprehends the criminals and turns them over to Inspector Peters.

Episode #9: "The Gumbo Man"
Original Broadcast Date: Saturday, August 6, 1949.
Plot: Jethro Dumont and Tulku venture to New Orleans, partly because the Green Lama was to give a lecture titled "The Effect of the Himalayas on Tibetan Philosophy," and meets Robert Frisbee, the famous historian. Frisbee's secretary, Pauline Evans, a petite blonde who's bright as a whip, vanished three days ago. The police have been on it since day two but haven't learned anything. While in search of a photograph of Pauline, Dumont and Tulku witness two murders.

THE LEGENDARY LYDECKER BROTHERS

JAN ALAN HENDERSON

The book is a 7x10 trade paperback, 196 pages, and retails for $24.95 (plus $5.05 s/h). Submit mail orders to Michael Bifulco, 1708 Simmons NE, Grand Rapids, MI 49505. For more information, email Michael Bifulco at mjbbooks5@comcast.net

It seems someone doesn't want her found. There are three suspects in the case: Achille, the gumbo man, who probably never heard of Pauline Evans; Eddie Damon, who wants to see Pauline Evans for business purposes; and Yvonne Perrin, who once hired Pauline and hasn't seen her in months. After discovering a map in Frisbee's missing book that reveals the location of the hidden gold of Jean Lafitte, Jethro has the gumbo man take him to the swamp to catch Yvonne Perrin in the act of removing the gold. Yvonne posed as Pauline Evans in order to get the information needed to retrieve the treasure. After sneaking up on the woman and stealing her gun, the Green Lama apprehends the murderer.

Episode #10: "The Adventure of the White Lady"
Original Broadcast Date: Saturday, August 13, 1949.
Plot: Flying back to New York from a recent visit to the island city of Havana, Jethro Dumont and Tulku are forced to bring along a stowaway—a small white Chihuahua. Arriving in New York, they are surprised to find the dead body of the dog's owner, Juan Martinez, in the cargo hold of the plane. Two men, Garfield Brommel and Manfred Thomas, attempt to learn the location of the White Lady, believing Dumont is in possession of the valuable diamonds. In an effort to discover what the White Lady is, Dumont searches for Nina Martinez, the niece of the dead man. After Nina is shot dead, Dumont solves the mystery. The White Lady is a gorgeous white sapphire, embedded in the rubber of the dog's toy bone. After the thieves have a falling out, the Green Lama apprehends the survivors of the double cross and turns them over to Lt. Harlow of the New York Police. The star sapphire is turned over to a U.S. Customs Inspector.

Episode #11: "The Case of the Perfect Prisoner"
Original Broadcast Date: Saturday, August 20, 1949.
Plot: Frank Cobb, an inmate at a prison in New York City, is about to receive the surprise of his life. Jethro Dumont helped with Cobb's rehabilitation by getting his sculptures shown in New York.

Arriving at the prison to be present when Cobb receives his pardon, the Lama is surprised to discover the dead body of Cobb, knifed in the back. Soon after, an attempted prison break occurs and the Green Lama manages to talk the inmates into dropping their weapons and coming out with their hands up. After further investigation, it appears (initially) that Cobb was responsible for smuggling the weapons into the prison. After questioning inmates like Sammy the Singer and Big Ben Hackett, Dumont finds Sammy's dead body stashed in a closet. It doesn't take long for the Green Lama to reveal to Warden Sandoe the guilty culprit. Captain Ed Summers smuggled the guns into the prison, hoping a prison break would cause the Warden to lose his job so that Summers could take his place. Confronted with the truth and disarmed, Summers is taken into custody.   *BT*

R. DeSoto

ARACHNID AGONY

The Passion of the Spider

BY WILL MURRAY

Spider-Man creator Stan Lee has been telling variations on this story for many years:

"Why Spider-Man? Simple. In the long-dead, practically Paleolithic era when I had been on the verge of approaching teenagerhood, one of my favorite pulp-magazine heroes was a stalwart named the Spider. He wore a slouch hat and a finger ring with the image of an arachnid—a ring which, when he punched a foe fearlessly in the face, would leave its mark, an impression of a spider. It was the Spider's calling card, and it sent goose pimples up and down my ten-year-old spine. More than that, I can still remember how the magazine's subtitle grabbed me. [The pulp] was called *The Spider*—but after his name were the never-to-be-forgotten words: *Master of Men*. . . . Now, as far as I can remember, the Spider had no superhuman powers. It seems to me he was just a good guy who fought the bad guys. It was his name that grabbed me. But that was enough."

It's difficult to imagine a hero less of a role model for Peter Parker than Richard Wentworth, the wealthy, chivalrous. aristocratic homicidal maniac known and feared as the Spider, Master of Men!

Writer Norvell W. Page described him this way:

For Richard Wentworth was a nemesis of the night, a swift and secret avenger who meted out lethal justice to those of the underworld who dared to raise their hand against humanity; he was the man known throughout half the civilized world as the Spider, and tonight he wore the disguise that would instantly identify him as that dread killer. A long, black cape covered twisted shoulders. A broad-brimmed hat tightly pulled down over a lank wig shadowed a beak-nosed face. The eyes that glittered there were steely with bitter hatred.

As for Wentworth himself, he believed it implicitly:

He was, he told himself, no longer a human being, but a cause. He was the Spider! He must live to defend humanity. . . .

Cloaked and be-hatted like The Shadow, the Spider was one of the night-prowling avengers who dominated the pulps during the 1930s. He resembled an anarchist, laughed like a maniac, and shot to kill.

Page often painted his hero in elevated terms:

Calm behind those wide-spaced eyes was such a brain as is given mankind only once in a generation, the brain that made him Master of Men, that inspired the genius-directed Crusades of Justice that had created the Spider … His exploits had raised him to the proportions of a legendary hero. In ancient times, Rome would have made him an emperor-god. Salem might have burned him as a sorcerer. The modern world—well, the police had offered rewards totaling thousands of dollars for his capture 'dead or alive.' And the Underworld hated him and plotted his destruction with a fierceness bred of abject terror.

Others times he just called a spade a spade.

Yes, Richard Wentworth was a murderer in the eyes of the law—a butcher who had slain a hundred, a thousand of his fellow men. They took no account of the fact he killed only those who richly deserved to die, that he alone had prevented a score of master criminals from overwhelming the forces of law and order.

Either way, his mission and methods remained the same. Take this slice of "Overlord of the Damned" (October 1935):

So Wentworth was constantly alert to detect the powerful evil men who arose now and again to harass mankind with megalomaniacal dreams of personal glory and bloody plunder. By his vigilance he had smashed Timurlanes who might have wrecked the world had they grown to full strength. And this long searching—this battling in the night—had taught him one very significant thing. Almost always, when such men arose, they were armed with some new and potent weapon— just as world history has been carved out by the most efficient killing implements. In this new use of an acid which not only maimed but killed the person on whom it was hurled, he sensed such a criminal weapon. Reading of the murders, he felt his whole body tense with the certainty that once more the underworld had arisen to kill, kill, kill!

The Spider believed in fighting fire with fire. His credo was an eye for an eye. Two pages later in the same story:

Wentworth ceased his fire, reloaded his guns, crawled further away from the wall which could splash liquid death down upon him. The Spider had known many horrors; he had grown cold to the incredible torturing deaths that the warped brains of criminals conceived; but this—this burning off of men's faces, this murder by torture—bred a red wrath in his soul. He wanted to stay here and kill, kill, kill.

"Kill, kill, kill" might have been the Spider's mantra. From "The Mayor of Hell" (January 1936):

His head ached splittingly, almost blinded him at every movement, but he could not delay now. If Kirkpatrick were not here, he must go to the second hideout and kill, kill, kill, until he had freed his friend.

But Wentworth had other slogans as well:

"Death is among you!" he cried. "The Spider brings death!"

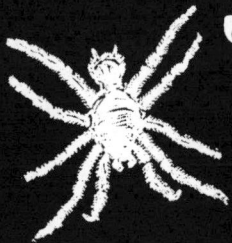

(And, more famously: "Death to the bringers of death!")

Once, when his friend and nemesis, Commissioner of Police Stanley Kirkpatrick, watched in awe as Wentworth outshot a half-dozen vicious foes without sustaining a scratch, he exclaimed, "They'll never kill you. You're immortal, a god, or at least a demi-god of battle. . . . "

The reader could easily believe it. With a "cold cosmic anger" in his eyes, his "eerie weapons of mercy" blasting away unerringly, the Spider seemed superhuman, shrugging off crippling bullet wounds and performing other feats of preternatural endurance that would have demolished an ordinary mortal. No wonder Page called him a "man of steel" four years before Superman debuted in the first issue of *Action Comics*.

Wentworth even possessed a kind of spider-sense:

And the Spider did not speak lightly of evil. He was too gentle, too tender a lover, to blot the glamorous night with useless vaporings. He was too courageous to take fright from vague notions. But through years of ceaseless struggle and hourly danger—not alone from the Underworld but also from the police who considered his brand-marked executions of criminals only murder—he had developed an uncanny feeling like the sixth sense of bats. Flying in the dark, scarcely seeing, the convoluted facial feelers of a bat received, apparently, an impact of air waves which forewarned the animal of obstacles in its path. So something—thought waves?—warned the Spider of danger.

It sounds more like Daredevil's radar sense than Spider-Man's famous spidey-sense. But like the latter, it reacted the same way:

Had the Spider been spotted? He couldn't be sure, but there was a tingling along his spine that seemed to warn of danger.

And Wentworth's own Spider-sense tingled often. Passages like this popped up frequently in Page's novels:

He felt a tingling race over his body as he studied the stubby, powerful build of the man, a tingling of apprehension. Cullihane's presence here spelled danger for all of them. . . . Wentworth's eyes tightened, his hands beneath the table clenched into hard knots. He was suddenly sure that his premonition was correct, that there would be slaughter here tonight. . . .

Premonitions often struck him forcefully. In Chapter One of "The Coming of the Terror" (September 1936), Wentworth is engaging in a little swordplay practice with his aide Jackson. . . .

Joy mounted within Wentworth, pumped jubilantly through his veins—and then, for no reason at all—he felt cold. The coldness touched his spine near its base, crept up toward his brain and spread tingling out over his shoulders, along his arms. And Jackson's questing point almost found his breast!

Sighting a liner steaming up the North River, another chill of dread comes over him. On no more than that, Wentworth tries withdrawing a ton of money from his bank. Too late. He's bankrupt. And before he knows it, the Living Pharaoh has descended upon New York City, plunging it into chaos. He had been a passenger on the Brittanic.

Yet there was a human side to this complex

man. Consider his strange relationship with semi-fiancée and series leading lady Nita van Sloan.

When he had met Nita, his life was already pledged to the service of humanity. The Spider had been a scourge of the Underworld for three full years. So he had fought against the love he knew could never reached culmination in marriage. What man could marry, have a home and children, when death and disgrace hung hourly over his head? No, he could not permit Nita to face such a possibility. He had told her that, long ago, when they found their love was stronger than the will to resist; had told her all his secret life in the hope that it might accomplish what his will had not. It had only drawn Nita closer to him, and they had fought the hard way together.

As Wentworth once remarked to her, "How perfectly is thy mystic karma attuned to mine!"

It's amazing to read of the real reason Wentworth yearned for a normal life during an intimate moment in "Slaves of the Dragon" (May 1936):

[Nita] . . . bowed her head to his shoulder, not crying, not doing anything but feeling his nearness to her. Wentworth's arms closed tightly and he stared out into the darkness of the street, his eyes wide and unseeing, a man would think the hurt would die after a while, the hurt of their barren lives. The fact that they could never be more than this to each other had been settled long, long ago. Marriage to both of them must mean the fulfillment of their love in children. Sharp laughter pushed against Wentworth's lips, but he choked it back. Could the Spider have children—the Spider upon whose shoulder the hand of the law, of disgrace, might drop heavily at any moment of the day or night? There had been moments when both of them had tried to forget

that, had turned their faces toward the ultimate happiness of their dreams. . . . Madness, utter madness.

But Wentworth's relationship with himself was far stranger. He himself once admitted, "There's a madness that gets in me when the Spider walks." Madness was a recurring theme. . . .

He looked down at his hand clenched hard about the newspaper, and for once in his vigorous life self-doubt arose to assail him. How many years was it now since first he had donned the valorous garments of the Spider? What sort of man had he become? But he knew without introspection. He was a man in whose hand a gun was more familiar than the hand-clasp of a friend, whose life was spent amid horror and death, whose eyes could never gaze upon a fellow man without probing behind the mask of humdrum existence and wondering: Shall I someday be forced to kill this man? If someone looked at him steadily or curiously, as had that guard upon the subway, he must immediately think that they had recognized him for what he was, that he was in peril of death or arrest through the agency of the person who looked. All this, merely that he might serve an ideal of justice.

Oh, there had been personal reasons behind his initial foray beyond the law—a dear friend was being framed out of life and honor and home. And there had been the example of his father, who had died when Wentworth was scarcely in his teens, a great lawyer murdered by criminals because he had dared defy them to save an innocent man they had made their scapegoat.

All of which sounds properly heroic, until you realize that less than a year before, Page blithely

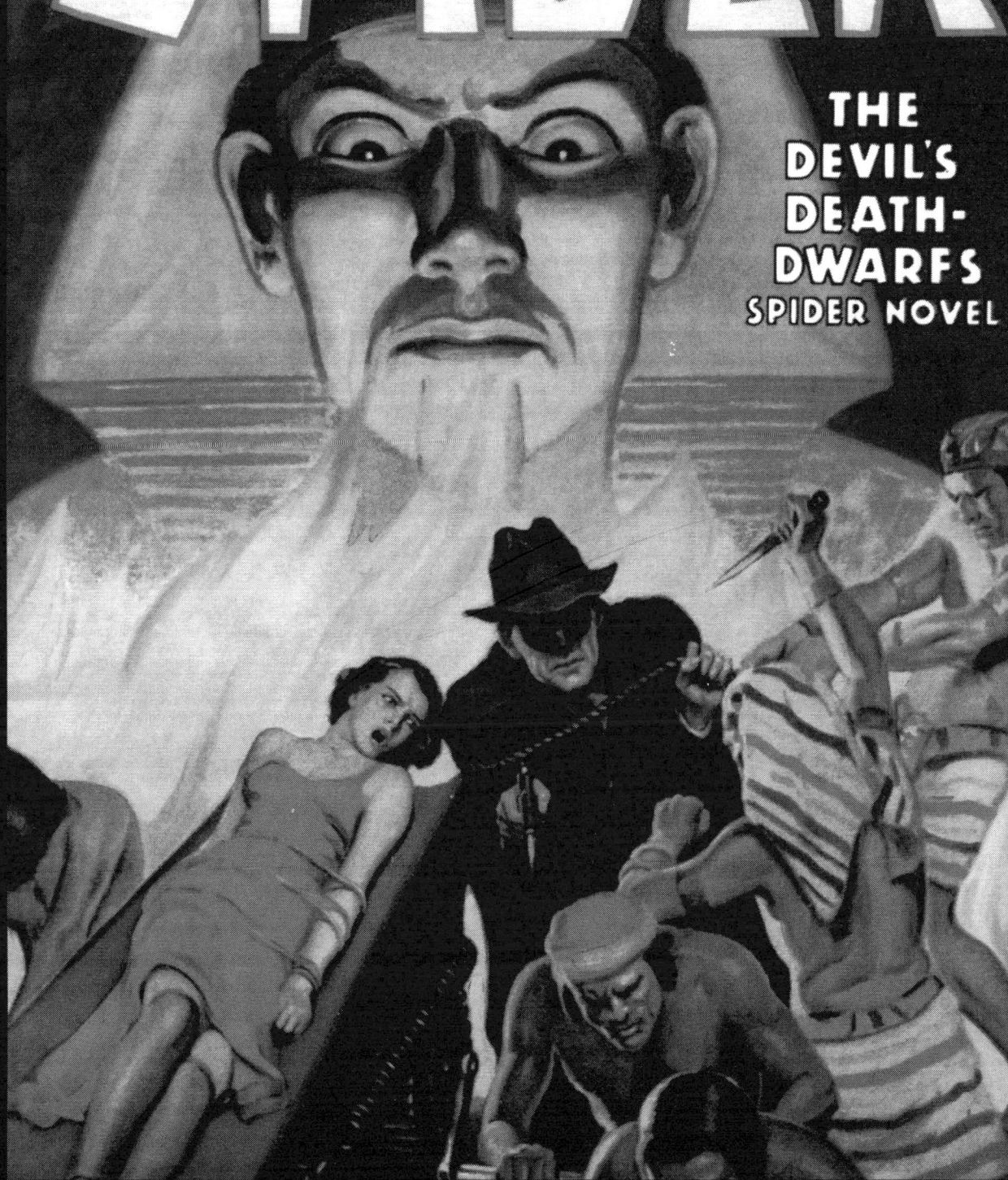

MASTER of MEN!

NRA

APRIL

THE

10¢

SPIDER

SLAVES
OF THE
CRIME
MASTER

FULL-LENGTH
SPIDER NOVEL

> **"He had plumbed the depths of despair, but always the cause of service had driven him on. Sometimes death seemed pleasant by contrast."**

informed *Spider* readers that Wentworth's parents had both died in an Alpine skiing accident when he was about ten. Or that in "Dragon Lord of the Underworld" (July 1935), Page assured rapt readers that the Spider's true self had lost his mother and father while he was in college. Their car had plunged off a bridge.

In "Slaves of the Crime Master" (April 1935), a more elevated reason for his becoming the Spider was offered:

> Wentworth had sworn his crusades of justice long ago solely because of his hatred of injustice, his great altruistic love for mankind.

Four chapters later, Page repeats the oft-told story that his hero was first motivated to become the Spider to rescue his mentor, Professor Brownlee from criminals, back in his college days. But then, consistency was a hallmark of neither Norvell Page nor Richard Wentworth. Consider this passage from "Builders of the Black Empire" (October 1934):

> Well, he had a system for getting out of even such fearful traps as this, a system that depended on his incredibly keen brain, on his super-trained body and mental reflexes. The system was simple. First, he never despaired. . . .

Skip ahead a year to:

> Wentworth set his Spider lips in hard determination. Stanley Kirkpatrick must answer to his friend tonight and he would find no mercy there, only the stern justice that he himself had more than once determined to mete out to the Spider. But there was in Wentworth's heart no sense of poetic justice. There was grief and pain and despair—but no lack of decision.

Or:

> Wentworth smiled sorrowfully. He had plumbed the depths of despair, but always the cause of service had driven him on. Sometimes death seemed pleasant by contrast.

Or:

> Despair flashed through Wentworth's heart. In a few moments, McRae would recover consciousness and, with his stubborn refusal to abandon ship, doom the thousand people whom Wentworth had risked so much to save. It was more than his own fate, if he failed to escape, which concerned the Spider in that moment.

Or:

> Wentworth was tortured by uncertainties and worries. Never before had a mass attack upon the country found him struggling so futilely for something against which to battle. Scores died daily under the suicide scourge of some megalomaniac criminal and the Spider—defender of distressed humanity—was helpless.

And:

> Wentworth was a gentle man by instinct. The arts held more appeal for him than for most other men. If he had not chosen the hard path of the Spider, he might have become the world's greatest virtuoso of the violin, a composer of note. Now and again, nature took this tool of the body and soul that he drove to such labors to exact the Spider's justice. Black despair. . . .

Life got even blacker for Wentworth in the ensuing years. Truth is, he despaired a lot. His darkest hour would be hard to identify—there were so many—but certainly in "The Coming of the Terror" he came near the bottom:

A great wave of weariness and an aching pain flooded Wentworth as he carried Nita, still struggling violently, to a bed and bound her helpless with wide bands from blankets. He stood looking down at her impotent rage throughout long moments of black despair.

And:

Wentworth felt the stiffness go out of his spine, and black despair churned in his brain.

Well, a lot of hemoglobin had washed under the bridge by that time, so perhaps this is not so much inconsistency as character development.

Once, during a respite in the novel of carnage called "Master of the Death-Madness" (August 1935), Kirkpatrick ticked off a long list of suspects. Wentworth blurted out the self-revealing truth. "I'm suspicious of everyone," he admitted, "even of myself sometimes."

And well he should have been. For Richard Wentworth was an undiagnosed manic-depressive—if not paranoid schizophrenic—subject to violent mood swings, climbing to unutterable heights of exultation in one scene, then crashing into the blackest depths of despair the next. When the Spider-madness came over him, he might pick up his treasured Stradivarius violin and launch into a nightlong serenade to soul-searching. Or, he might putty up his face, don black hat and cape, go out Spidering . . .

Virtually every Spider novel contained a scene where Richard Wentworth slipped into a secret room in his Manhattan digs, there to eradicate his handsome features:

His deft fingers flew swiftly about their familiar task. Under their touch, a lotion tautened his skin so that it shone across the cheekbones and became darkly sallow. Circles now appeared under his eyes, and his lips vanished, leaving his mouth a sinister, knife-thin line. That was all, except a reconstruction of the nose so that it became a hooked predatory beak, crowned by harsh, shaggy eyebrows, all topped by a lank, long wig, while the face that stared back at Wentworth bore no resemblance at all to the debonair countenance of Richard Wentworth, clubman, dilettante of the arts, and amateur criminologist. This was a face from whose glare the criminal guiltily shrank as from a death ray! This was the face of the Spider!

If he was feeling particularly predatory, Wentworth added a pair of celluloid vampire fangs. An artificial hump under his coat was calculated to suggest a human arachnid. Clearly, this was not a typical Park Avenue *bon vivant*.

For one thing, he seemed pathologically obsessed with branding his kills with the scarlet seal of the Spider. No matter how much it risked life, limb, and exposure of his most dangerous secret, never mind that he was surrounded by the hounds of the law, baying for his blood, Wentworth could never resist pressing the base of his platinum cigarette lighter to a cold criminal cranium, adding yet another reason for the State for strap him into the electric chair.

Wentworth had forgotten that he wore the damning robes of the Spider, that three men back there in that den of battle bore his mocking seal upon their foreheads; he had forgotten that the police were here, hot upon his heels by this time, that the lives of thousands of his countrymen depended upon him.

THE SPIDER

MASTER OF MEN!

10¢ SEPTEMBER

THE
CORPSE
BROKER

Book-Length
Spider Novel
by GRANT
STOCKBRIDGE

MASTER of MEN!

THE
10¢ SPIDER

OCT.

HIS PAST VICTORIES OVER CRIME-
DOM RETURN TO PLAGUE THE
SPIDER—WHEN HE IS ATTACK-
ED BY A COMBINATION OF HIS
OLDEST AND DEADLIEST ENEMIES

THE COUNCIL OF EVIL
BOOK-LENGTH ANTI-CRIME SAGA
by GRANT STOCKBRIDGE

Once while waiting in ambush, Wentworth noticed a problem with one of his weapons and grew reflective:

The barrel, when he glanced through it, was dark with powder stain. It needed cleaning badly. He thoughtfully reversed his guns, putting the dirty one under his right arm. How many men had those ready guns of his destroyed? On how many foreheads had he printed the red seal of his justice? His eyes widened a little. By the gods, he had even lost count of the number of the . . . executions . . . he had performed.

Was it possible that a man could kill and kill until he lost all sense of the value of human life?. . . . His cigarette sent up threads of smoke, unnoticed between his gloved fingers. He was thinking of death. How many times he had dared the sweep of the Grim Reaper's keen blade? Had even known the coldness as of its black night . . . How many men, yes and women, too, he had sent to stare into the eyeless sockets of death . . . !

Nita van Sloan seemed to recognize the precarious mental tightrope her Dick walked:

She was coaxing him, trying to turn his thoughts aside from the grimness for a while, his thoughts which too often were dread and somber things dwelling on death and vengeance and wholesale destruction. There had been times when Nita had feared that his mind might dwell too long on blood and horror. There was in her memory the fact that genius, of whatever kind, is often too close to madness. And there was no disputing that this man of hers was a veritable god of battles, a master of men. . . .

A Master of Men, perhaps, but hardly a master of himself. At the slightest hint, he would turn on his close friends, accusing them of gross betrayal. And if he ever felt they had gone bad . . . well, Wentworth set himself up in his own mind as judge, jury and executioner. His best friend, Commissioner Kirkpatrick, pointedly told him that he would send Richard Wentworth to the death house if positive proof that he was the Spider ever came into his hands. Once, Kirkpatrick actually did. And Wentworth admired him for it.

And woe unto him who trespassed on the Spider's unlawful preserves. In "The Council of Evil" (October 1940), Wentworth interrupts a gang of teenagers beating up a racketeer. When they protest, Wentworth admonishes them. "You were taking the law in your own hands! That is not the American way!"

When they point out that the Spider doesn't go to the police, Wentworth replies. "You're not the Spider, son. The Spider has devoted his entire life to crime detection. He is a qualified judge. And he never strikes . . . unless the police have failed."

For Richard Wentworth saw himself as a man on a holy mission. A self-appointed messiah with a martyr complex. A Christ covered in cobwebs:

He was the champion of oppressed humanity, its shield and protector against the murderous outbreaks of the underworld; wherever crime struck terribly, that way he hastened, taking up the challenge. The police had offered rewards totaling thousands of dollars for his capture "dead or alive." And the underworld hated him, and plotted his destruction with a fierceness bred of abject terror.

But the Spider was indifferent alike to proscription by the underworld and dogged persecution by police. Evading their bullets and traps, he continued to fight his thankless battle as humanity's paladin. . . .

And he seemed to rejoice in being outnumbered by impossible odds. Captured by a modern-day buccaneer in "Pirates from Hell" (August 1940), Wentworth eschewed his usual black despair:

> One man against more than a hundred pirates, of course, a hundred killers. The Spider knew that, but it did not check the wild impulse to laughter that squeezed his lungs,
>
> It was no wonder that men call the Spider mad!

Yes, no wonder at all.

Norvell Page churned out the Spider's adventures for three white-hot years, then dropped from sight in the middle of the four-part "Living Pharaoh" series (after completing "The Devil's Death Dwarfs" for the October 1936 issue), not to return until mid-1937. No one today can say exactly what happened, but hints I've picked up suggest a nervous breakdown of some kind. God knows, you could see it coming in his alter ego, Richard Wentworth.

Early in 1936, the *American Fiction Guild Bulletin* reported that "Norv" Page was now down to 200 pounds, and "back in his old tempo." His byline was again popping up in various mags. This certainly hints that he'd been on a health sabbatical.

In the autumn of 1939, Page took an ocean cruise on doctor's orders, and almost had another nervous breakdown, this time in mid-ocean. World War II had just broken out and passenger liners were suddenly at risk of being torpedoed by enemy U-boats. He recovered well enough and settled down to keeping *The Spider* going, but World War II and its paper shortages took their toll—causing Popular Publications to fold the magazine in 1943 after ten years and two months of bullet-punctuated fury. The house name of Grant Stockbridge, under which Page and his substitutes wrote the character's exploits, was solemnly retired. And then, finally, Norvell Page, grieving the tragic death of his wife, joined *Shadow* ghostwriter Theodore Tinsley in making his way to Washington D. C, where both men toiled for the duration in the Office of War Information. As far as anyone knows, neither wrote a line of pulp after 1943.

Almost 70 years after the last original Spider novel was published, the Master of Men lives on in new stories and comic books, with the original 110 novels reaching younger audiences in a variety of reprints and being made into audiobooks and even e-Books. The hero neither the underworld nor the police could kill is proving to be immortal . . . or at least exceedingly hard to kill. *BT*

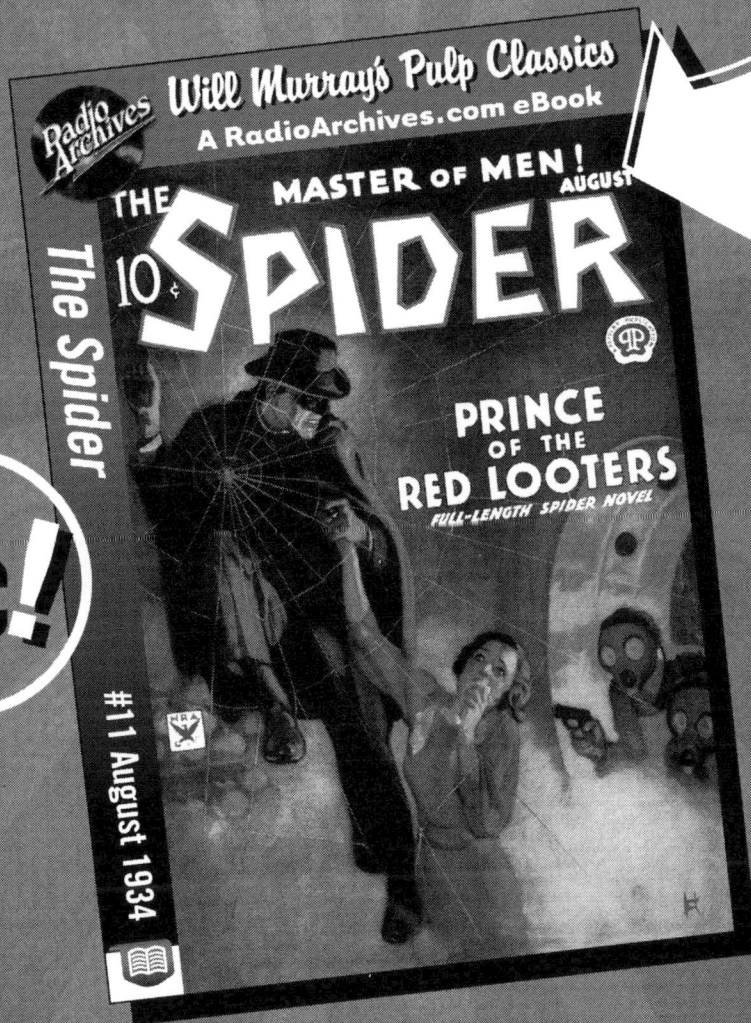

THE MOBSTER MAN

by WILLIAM E. BARRETT

THE NEWS sheets of the old town were dull as only newspapers can be dull in the days and the weeks when crime news lags. The underworld like a gorged python lay coiled upon itself waiting. There were elections coming up and there was a big graft investigation under way. The politicians were busy and gang guns cooled while mobsters laid low.

Dean Culver thumbed the sheets over indifferently. He had been back in town more than a month, back after a year of exile. He stopped turning pages when he came to the first page of the *Press-Courier's* second edition. The banner spot on that page was the two column feature under a cryptic head "The Blue Barrel." Culver smiled grimly.

That heading was his idea and the column was his idea and only he

A COMPLETE NOVELETTE

"Come on in," growled that hard voice as the gun prodded Culver's back. "We'll have a real party now."

The "Blue Barrel" erupted hot lead and information—which was the most deadly was a question unanswered until Dean Culver wrote the solution in fiery letters on the heart of those who wore the double cross as a badge of honor.

knew it. The *Press-Courier* itself did not know where the phoned items came from; the *Press-Courier* knew only that the whispering voice on the phone was the hottest tipster on the underworld that the town had ever known. What Winchell had done for Broadway, The Blue Barrel was doing for the underworld of another city. The *Press-Courier* took its increased circulation gratefully, featured the column and forebore curiosity.

But the *Press-Courier* had fired Dean Culver over a year before. It had fired him and turned him out disgraced after an underworld frame. A Cordo gangster had died under the guns and there had been "evidence" in his effects that branded Culver as a crooked reporter. He had been through then and he had got out. Now he was back. His lips thinned.

The man who had framed him was the town's big political poobah, "Black Bart" Brunderson. Culver had played too hard. Well, he was playing harder now and the "Blue Barrel" was his weapon. As the blue barrel of an automatic might stand for death, the blue barrel of the *Press-Courier* stood for exposure. And Dean Culver was shooting the deadly paragraphs. He was not a stool and the "square crooks" did not tempt his aim. It was too bad for the chiselers, though, and he was biding his time until the day when he could get Black Bart in the sights.

For several minutes he read, then he yawned and turned in. He had the faculty of dropping off to sleep immediately. He did not know exactly when he awakened. Something had stirred in the room. He lay motionless in the pulsating darkness. Cautiously, his hand crept along the coverlet until he felt the cold butt of his automatic under the pillow. Something moved in the shadows near the window.

"That's enough, you mugg! I've got the drop."

CULVER'S voice slashed through the brooding darkness that had settled after that one slithering sound. He heard a faint gasp from the shadows and his hand darted to the light socket beside his bed. Light flooded the room and Culver, eyes squinted against the sudden glare, saw a shabby little man who pressed back against the window with arms outstretched. The intruder's face was pasty white and covered with unkempt gray stubble. Faded, washed out eyes pleaded silently. The man's mouth worked.

"I didn't—"

"Shut up! I'll do the talking."

Culver slid cautiously out of bed. His eyes ranged the room and lingered for a moment on the partly open window. He frowned. It was a good ten yards along a narrow cornice from the fire escape to that window. He looked again at the shabby stranger. It seemed inconceivable that such a poor specimen could have made the cat walk.

"All right," he said, "I'll listen to what you've got to say."

The intruder wet his lips. "I'm Beau Bridwell," he said. There was pride in the statement and the mere act of mentioning the name seemed to steady the man. He brushed his lips again. "You're Dean Culver, aren't you? I didn't make a mistake?"

Culver nodded. "I'm Culver and you made a helluva mistake."

"No. No." Bridwell looked around like a trapped animal. "I had to see you. Doc Bromley told me when I was going out that you were square. I had to see you and—"

"Yeah?" Culver was interested but he had no intention of letting the other know it. Doc Bromley had been a pretty decent crook and Culver had given him a good press when he got in trouble. "You had to see me, so you jimmied in. Swell. They've got doors on this joint."

"Sure." Bridwell's lips twisted. "It would look good for you, too, if I walked in and paid a visit." He laughed harshly. "When half the town is goin' to be hot on my trail tomorrow—"

"What for?"

Bridwell's face seemed whiter than ever. He wet his lips again. "I just left Judge O'Ryan's house. He sent me over for a double saw buck when he was trial judge and I swore I'd kill him if I ever got out. The papers published it when I said it." He took a deep breath. "Well, the Judge is dead."

Culver's eyes widened. *"You killed O'Ryan!"*

"No. No. I swear I didn't." Bridwell was trembling again. "I was in the house but I never touched him—"

"Sit down. I want details—and fast." Culver moved to the window, looked out along the narrow ledge and then crossed to the door. Satisfied that no one else was showing any exceptional interest in his affairs he came back and sat down. Bridwell was fumbling with a cigarette.

"The governor gave me a pardon last Tuesday," he said dazedly. "A full pardon. The papers raised hell. Seems like the same day he signed the pardon, there was a meeting of the parole board and they voted nix on giving me a parole."

"I read about that. Go on."

"Well, I was just as balled up as the sheets and I've been wondering ever since. I didn't have no mouthpiece working for a pardon, no politics in back o' me and no dough. Howcome, then, I get pardoned when the governor's running for re-election and giving me a pardon means him getting hell from the papers?"

"I'll bite. Why? But get along to this O'Ryan killing."

BEAU BRIDWELL shivered slightly. "I don't believe in nothing that I don't understand," he said slowly. "That there pardon o' mine was screwy somehow and I got worried. I figured maybe O'Ryan was back of it and had maybe some new facts or something—"

"Yeah? Did you do the job that you went up for?"

Bridwell shifted uneasily. Dean Culver waved. "Okay. You were guilty as hell. Go on."

"Well, there ain't nobody better at opening up a box than I am, even if I'm out of practice." Beau Bridwell's thin shoulders squared. "And I figured maybe there'd be a tipoff in O'Ryan's safe on why I got that pardon. It had me screwy worrying about it being some kind of frame and I had to know."

Culver nodded, his eyes narrowed. He could understand that. Bridwell took a deep breath. "I jimmied in as easy as buyin' a drink but I wasn't no more than in the place when I hears a noise and it's between me and my getaway. I fade out into a dark hall and then I hear somebody moving upstairs, too. There ain't no place for me to go, so I back into a little mop closet under the stairs and just wait. Then I hear somebody comin' down the stairs and he goes right into the study where I'd just left; the place where the safe is. There's a lot o' quick action in there and he gets the light on; then I hear him give a quick choking kind of sound and he falls. I can hear his body hit."

Beau Bridwell wiped his forehead. "That was just hell for me. I figure that it's the judge that's come down the stairs and here I am in his place when he gets socked; me, the guy that swore to kill him.''

"Yeah. That's exciting. How did you know he was killed?"

"I looked in afterwards. They was awful still for a while and then when nobody else showed up, they started to move around again. There was two fellers in there and maybe three. I crawled to the door and the judge was sprawled out on the floor. There was a lantern on the floor in front of the safe and a feller working for the combination. Me, I crawled up the stairs and found a window that went out on a porch. Then I came here—''

Dean Culver was jumping into his clothes. "You mugg! Taking all that time to come to the point and those crumbs still working on that safe. Hells bells!''

Bridwell's jaw dropped. "What are you going to do?"

"Do? I'm going out there. Here, throw these on. Fit you too much but that's all right."

Culver tossed a well worn suit across to the bewildered Bridwell. He flipped a pair of twenty dollar bills after it. "When you get those rags on, drift right out the front way like you owned the place. Do a quick blow to Mother Mason's. You know it, don't you?"

The little crook's nod was enough. Most old timers knew Mother Mason's. Culver was slipping on the harness that held his armpit holster close to his body.

"Okay. Mother Mason's. And keep your mouth shut. Give her *both those twenties* and tell her I sent you. Then wait! You interest me and maybe I'll go all the way with you."

A quick flip set his gray felt in place and he snapped the brim; then he was gone. Beau Bridwell wet his lips.

CHAPTER TWO

THE MURDER ROOM

THE HOME of Judge Michael J. O'Ryan was a gloomy pile of gray stone that stood in an acre of ground just inside the City line. Culver slipped through the row of trees that paralleled the auto driveway and circled to the back of the house; every sense alert to signs of alarm either inside or outside the house. The judge, he knew, was a widower who kept only two aged servants in the old house and a chauffeur who slept over the garage. There was little chance of the murder being discovered until morning as long as it had not already been discovered. Still, it was not a sure bet. He circled the house warily before he moved on the window in back through which Bridwell had entered.

He had no intention of stepping into a trap at the scene of a murder, but he had a powerful urge to visit the scene before the police tracked up the place. He hardly dared to hope that the safe had proved tough and that the intruders would be still there—if they had ever been there —but he granted that it would be more than interesting to come across the men at work.

For Culver knew—as all the city knew—that Judge O'Ryan had spent nearly six months digging up evidence of graft and corruption on the state government in its dealings with the municipality. Quite conceivably, there were a number of persons who would breathe easier if the Judge breathed no more.

Not a sound disturbed the suburban quiet of two A. M. as Culver tested the window. It moved easily under his hand and it was only the work of seconds to raise it and step over the sill. Then, in the black darkness of the old house, he stood and listened. Somewhere a clock was ticking noisily and he could hear the insignificant sound of water dripping somewhere from an imperfectly closed tap. Other than that, he was alone with the beating of his own heart. He glided forward, his eyes accustomed now to the darkness, and found himself in a big room that was probably the dining room. At the far end there was a door leading off a hall. He stepped through and crouched low when he saw the stairway. His eyes narrowed.

There was a little mop room under the stairs just as Bridwell had said, but it was much easier to get out by way of the window which he had used as an entrance than it was to go upstairs.

At the foot of the stairs and to the left, there was an open door and Culver moved toward it cautiously. His hand closed over the butt of his gun and he balanced lightly on his feet, then he looked in. Darkness shrouded the room but he didn't need light to tell him the obvious thing. There was no one in there.

Some of the tension went out of Culver then and he stepped into the room. His hand found the flash on his right hip and he turned it toward the floor. A little circle of light stabbed the darkness; darkness that suddenly became a tangible, living thing; black shuddering gloom that pressed upon the challenging beam of light and struggled to engulf it,

to hide from it the thing that lay on the floor.

Sprawled there on the floor just two steps in from the hall lay the body of a man, his arms spread wide, fingers clutching emptiness.

CULVER'S lips tightened in a straight line and he dropped to one knee. The man's face was almost buried in the thick nap of the rug and Culver moved him gently. The pencil-thin beam of light moved over rigid features, strong even in death, across the sparse gray hair and then stopped. High up on the man's head was a horrible wound; horrible because the skull had not withstood the blow.

"The Judge all right. Bashed his skull in. Never knew what hit him. Length of gas pipe maybe." He was puzzled at the manner of the murder. The job did not look modern. It didn't have the professional touch.

"I wonder now. I wonder." He moved across the room and located the wall safe. His flash played over it and he recognized it as a good one. It showed no evidence of having been worked on. Not a scratch violated its shiny surface. He tried it with a gloved hand. The door was locked. He circled the floor about the safe with the probing flash but found nothing significant. Once more he let the flash wink out and sat down in a big chair.

His nerves were tense, but he felt that he was on the verge of drawing cards in a very big game and that he was justified in staying on the premises until he had checked all the angles. There was a chance of police interference, but the chance was so slim that he discounted it. They wouldn't show until someone called them. If they did—well, that would be too bad.

"Either that mug, Bridwell, was so scared he got mixed up or he deliberately lied. Why?"

Culver let his eyes wander in the direction of the hall door. He couldn't figure any reason for Bridwell going up-stairs to get out of the house. "Any jury would hang him," he said slowly, "and I don't know but what I would, too. There could have been three other fellows here —but were there?"

He got up and crossed the room toward the body and then stopped with a jerk; every faculty suspended, a strange crawling sensation running along the surface of his skin.

The tomb-like stillness of this room of death was being shattered by the shrill, clamorous ringing of the telephone.

For the space of a heart beat, Dean Culver stood rooted; then he took a quick step toward the desk and lifted the receiver. There was no conscious reasoning in the decision; sheer instinct warned him that the ringing of that bell would bring the household and that he would be trapped—or given at best a short start on the baying hounds of the law. For all he knew, of course, the damage was already done, but he had to risk that.

"Judge O'Ryan's residence." His voice was well under control.

"Long Distance. Capitol City calling Judge O'Ryan."

"Sorry. His honor cannot be disturbed."

"Wait a minute." The girl's voice seemed to fade out, then he heard her in a sort of faraway conversation. "Sorry, sir. They say that Judge O'Ryan cannot be disturbed." Then a heavy, masculine voice cut in.

"This is Governor Barker. It is imperative that I speak to Judge O'Ryan at once."

CULVER'S eyes glistened with a strange intensity. He heard the girl ask the governor if he would speak to whoever was on the line and the sharp affirmative; then the voice was demanding.

"What is this about not disturbing the judge for a long distance call?"

"He left orders, sir." Culver was sparring for time. He felt as though he were chained to that murder room by the slender thread of wire. To hang up would be to direct instant suspicion or—the phone would start jangling again.

"Orders be hanged. This is Franklin Barker speaking, Governor Barker. Do you understand?"

"Yes, sir."

"Say, who is this?" There was suspicion in the governor's voice. Culver took a deep breath. He might, he decided, gain a few precious minutes by a bold stroke.

"This," he said slowly, "is somebody who has no business in Judge O'Ryan's residence. I came here and found something that I had nothing to do with. Judge O'Ryan is lying dead in his study. He's been murdered."

He heard the governor's quick intake of breath and his swift ejaculation of shocked dismay. He waited for no more. The long distance operator was probably plugged in. Whether she was or not, it would not take long for the governor to raise the alarm. He whipped the receiver onto the hook and darted for the exit.

"I'd give something pretty to know what the governor wanted with O'Ryan at two-thirty in the A. M." he whispered. "There's a real angle to play on."

He was over the window ledge with one quick writhing motion and the tree shadows swallowed him as he made his way rapidly to the car that he had parked two blocks from the grim stone house. As the powerful motor whirred him toward town, he could hear the police sirens wailing. He smiled cynically.

A murder was about to be officially discovered.

Two minutes later he was in the phone booth of an all night drug store and a frantic staff at the *Press-Courier* was tearing up the Home Final that would be at every door in the morning. The two column strip from section two was being slapped around and the Blue Barrel was on the front page with another beat.

CHAPTER THREE

At Zoro's

THE DAWN was still an hour and a half away when Culver stepped down a short flight of steps to the basement entrance of a once magnificent residence. A door swung open and the sounds of music drifted along the dimly lighted passageway that led to the rear of the house.

To the public, this place was Diamond Dan's; a place where one might dine and dance and drink better than average liquor at any hour of the night, a deluxe spot that had never felt the heavy hand of the raiders nor the fetid breath of scandal—in short, a well-nigh perfect speakeasy. To the underworld, this was "Big John Zoro's," a place run on the "Word of a Sicilian." It was out of bounds as far as the police were concerned and no man, no matter how badly wanted, was subject to the fear of arrest while he was on the premises; by the same token, gangsters might take their ease in the same room with sworn enemies and not fear lead. It was a confidential place and things might be arranged there. It was, in short, the pulse beat of the underworld and the man who knew how to read significance in little things might forecast the future from a ringside table at Big John's.

Culver was interested in the underworld's pulse rate tonight. The murder of Judge O'Ryan was going to rock the crime world to its foundations and the smart members would be drifting in for veiled discussion. He did not, however, get his ringside table.

Big John himself bore down upon him as he stepped into the big room. "Ah, Culver, my frien'. I am glad to see you in-a my place. Always I am-a glad to see you—"

"Yeah. That's the old come-on baloney for the suckers, John. What's on your mind?"

Big John seemed pained. He shrugged a fat pair of shoulders. Careful barbering had not taken the greasiness out of his skin and there was a dirty stream of perspiration rolling down his fleshy cheek. He passed his fingers lightly across his full mustache and the gesture seemed to wipe away the grimness that had lingered momentarily in his face. He grinned widely.

"Always you joke, Culver. That is fine. Me, I laugh and kid with everybod'. Sure Mike. Fine feller with all the boys— Smile all the time, that's a-me, Zoro.''

"I'll sign a paper and swear that's right; but spit out the works, John. What's the lay.''

Zoro's manner became confidential. He leaned forward. "Some good friends of yours, Culver, they want they should see you in room 'C.' Right away they want they should see you.''

Dean Culver's eyes narrowed. "Spill the names, John.''

Zoro shrugged. "The boss,'' he said. "The Mister Brunderson.''

Culver digested that. He nodded his head. "Much obliged. I'll go right up, John.''

The Sicilian grinned and bobbed his head. He seemed relieved as he hastened away to spread the glad hand to some new arrivals. Culver lighted a cigarette and inhaled slowly.

"The old sinner knew that there wasn't any friendship in that call from 'C', '' he said. "He kind of hated to give me the message. Oh, well. We'll look.''

HE STROLLED slowly to the stairs. At the head of the short flight, he turned into the long dim passageway and paused outside of the door marked "C.'' He took out a fresh cigarette, stuck it in his mouth and held a cigar lighter in his hand as he rapped on the door.

It opened wide and he smiled grimly as he looked into the eyes of the man who opened it; Vito Torino, boss of the city's second largest mob. The only other person in the room was Black Bart Brunderson, the political power behind many thrones. Culver dropped his lighter into his pocket, took out a match and lighted his cigarette. He nodded indifferently to Torino and fixed his eyes on Black Bart.

"Heard you were looking for me. Right?''

Heavy jawed, slightly bald and larded with a good forty pounds of excess weight, Black Bart was a formidable figure. He was rolling an unlighted cigar along his lips and his eyes were drawn in behind narrow slits in the big pouches that surrounded them. Torino, a beautifully barbered youth, closed the door softly. Brunderson grunted.

"We been talking about you, Culver. We ain't sure we like you.''

"No? That's a damn shame, Brunderson.''

"No foolin', it's a shame.'' Brunderson's cigar stood straight out from suddenly tightened lips. "O'Ryan got the bump tonight, Culver, and that raises hell. This here is a census. You were washed up on the news sheets a year ago. What's your racket?''

Culver's eyes were narrowed. "Do I have to have one?''

Brunderson glared. The cigar did a quick, rolling round trip along his wet lips. "The waltz don't get you anything,'' he said. "You play around the hot spots and you're working for something or somebody. You don't print your dough. You'll either lay your cards on the table with me, Guy, or you'll find you're in the wrong town. Get it?''

Culver let the smoke curl lazily from his nostrils. His eyes held Brunderson's. "What will happen?''

It was like a slap in the face. Black Bart straightened. His fist hit the table. "Happen? You lame-brained punk! Everybody knows you ain't regular. Everybody knows that the papers are off you. What does it leave? Bah! You know what happens to stool-pigeons."

Culver laughed. "Come again. You know I'm not a stool and you didn't get where you are by taking wild swings in the dark. What else have you got that I'd be interested in?"

Vito Torino cut in before the apoplectic Boss could answer. His voice was soft. "You mus' not play the damn fool, Culver. Always when a man will not do business, there is the bump—"

The air of easy badinage that he had worn in dealing with Black Bart dropped from Culver as he whirled toward the gang leader. His eyes bored into the little wop who played the cards of double-cross and murder for high stakes.

"That's just fine, Vito," he said crisply. "There's a phone down the hall. You call up Pete Cordo and tell him that you are going to put Dean Culver on the spot. Go ahead. Call him!"

THE GANGSTER wet his lips and looked toward Brunderson. He made no move toward the phone. Culver laughed and turned to the door. "Glad to've seen you boys," he said. The door slammed.

Outside in the discreetly dim hall, however, Culver was not smiling. He took two steps, doubled back and leaned against the door of the room that he had just quitted. He heard Brunderson's booming voice.

"Why didn't you call Pete Cordo?"

Then the shrill, womanish voice of the excited Vito. "Not me, Boss. This Culver he must not be bumped. Cordo says that. Some day if you and me—"

The voice dropped, faded out. Culver glided away, hesitated at the head of the stairs and then walked down confidently. The big room was filling up. There was the usual quota of hilarious parties and a more than normal number of quiet, hard eyed men who sat at tables without women. Culver took a table in the corner and ordered dinner. His mouth was hard.

It was a tough spot. No matter how lightly he may have taken it in Brunderson's presence, it was not funny now. Culver had been biding his time against a clash with Brunderson. He wanted power in his hands next time and he was not ready yet. Brunderson still held the power that a politician always holds; the power of the frame. And Brunderson had an ally now with another kind of power; the power of the Tommy gun.

Between Culver and the first danger, there was nothing but his own wits. Between Culver and the guns of Vito Torino's mob, there stood only Pete Cordo. And Pete Cordo had reason to hate Culver as much as he feared him.

Culver had an idea that his mention of Cordo had been a mistake. He shook his head grimly and looked up.

Black Bart Brunderson was swinging across the big room alone; headed for the door. Culver's eyes narrowed. He had a sudden hunch to follow along and acted on it. Brunderson was going through the wide doors in front when Culver stood up.

CHAPTER FOUR

TWENTY-FOUR HOURS TO LIVE

CULVER came briskly up the steps from Zoro's and hesitated at street level. He had lost Brunderson. A long dark sedan moved from the curb half way up the block and moved toward the spot where Culver stood.

It moved like the shadow of death itself and he had no time to get under cover. His hand darted to his armpit and he crouched back against the building front. A voice snarled from the shadows:

"None o' that. Walk out nice."

He was covered. He turned his head slightly toward the voice, then swept his eyes front. He couldn't see the man who had spoken and the car was in front of him now. He drew a deep breath and stepped out. A man stepped out from the shadows behind him and stuck a gun in his spine. He moved toward the car. Pete Cordo glared out at him. Beside the big shot of gangdom sat Bart Brunderson. Culver let his breath out slowly. This wasn't a bump then; this was an inquisition. He bowed mockingly. Brunderson was grinning.

"I been telling Pete how you're goin' around braggin' that there ain't nobody big enough to bump you off."

Culver looked at him coolly. The lights in front of Big John's were bright enough to allow him to read faces. "Have I been bragging?"

"You told me that Pete Cordo wouldn't let you get bumped, didn't you? That's bragging. There was a vicious intensity in Black Bart's voice. Culver turned to Pete Cordo. "I told that cheap little perfumed cannon o' Brunderson's—Vito Torino—that he couldn't do it," he said slowly. "Am I right or wrong, Pete?"

Cordo had a broad, Slavic, unintelligent face. He frowned and shifted uneasily. "Nobody talks for Pete Cordo. I don't let nobody say what I will do." He didn't look at Culver. Brunderson cut in fast.

"You're probably holding something Pete wants, Culver," he said. "But that won't get you anything with me and Pete working together. You're going to spit clean about who you're working for or you're taking a long ride. Pete's not backing you worth a damn."

Culver shrugged. He did have something on Cordo and he had not hesitated to use it in a world where men fought with any weapon at hand. He would have scorned to take blackmail money, but he had needed the security that had been his by virtue of Pete Cordo's fear. Now that security was being threatened and his life wasn't good for an hour under present circumstances with the hand of Pete Cordo against him.

He had seconds to come to a decision about Brunderson and his interest in the affair. Brunderson lived for politics and he lived for power. He was not taking a lot of time tonight, of all nights, on the affairs of Dean Culver unless he, too, was afraid; afraid that Culver's racket was political. Black Bart's activity tonight was a giveaway. He had something at stake, something with which he feared interference.

In a flash, Culver's decision was made. If he was important to Brunderson, it was because Brunderson had a weakness in his armor some place. Brunderson was afraid, despite his bluster, and a man who has something big at stake and who fears to lose it is a prime customer for a good bluff. Culver's teeth flashed in a smile.

"I'm not walking away from here into any bump, Brunderson," he said softly, "for the same reason that I haven't been bumped before. Pete played the sucker by letting you get in on him, but Pete is still protecting me for the good of his own hide. Get that?"

BRUNDERSON rolled the cigar and turned to Pete Cordo. Cordo's face was sullen. He was between two fires and he was beginning to realize that he hadn't played the game like a big shot. It made him angry and red spots glowed in his cheeks. For the first time he met Culver's eyes. His brutal lips curled back from his teeth.

"Culver, you maybe haven't got what you say you've got. I got to see it. If you got it, you let me see it. If you don't let me see it—then by God, you have not got that thing!"

The words came hard as though pumped out by a brain unaccustomed to framing long sentences. Culver's lips thinned. "Cordo," he said bluntly, "you know what I think of you. You're a dumb mutt and not too terribly tough. But you're big, Cordo, because you keep your eye on the ball and you don't make the mistake of getting brainy. That ain't your game. You run your mob in words of one syllable and thoughts of one syllable. When you get in with a bird like Brunderson, you're hearing words you never heard before and you're getting

your brain into things it don't understand. Lay off!"

Black Bart's eyes widened and the cigar slipped from his lips. "What the hell—"

His voice trailed off. Pete Cordo had lifted his head and his eyes were flaming. Culver had played his cards well out of his knowledge of those who live by guns rather than gab. Pete Cordo could understand the double cross when he couldn't understand anything else. His mind, as elemental as an animal's, was easily reached by a suggestion of treachery. He was suspicious by nature; dull witted and painfully conscious of his mental inferiority. As Culver had pointed out, the very secret of his power lay in his dull mind. The agile brains of politicians had not been able to ensnare him because he had refused to engage in any duel of wits. Tonight he had departed from his custom because Brunderson had pretended to know more than he did know about Culver's hold on him; a bluff that the politician was already regretting. Cordo hadn't missed that crack about Torino either.

Brunderson was breathing hard, but fighting for the poise that is the armor of the Boss. He wasn't big for nothing. "Pete," he said, "this guy is one smart cookie. His one play was to get between us and he pulled it off. I pay off on him, but—"

Cordo waved him down. "Pete Cordo talks for Pete Cordo," he growled. He was no longer undecided. There was a heavy frown on his broad face. He leaned toward Culver and his eyes glittered.

"Culver," he said, "I have never see what you got. I mus' see it. If you got this thing, we talk business.

If not—" He spat. "I give you twenty-four hours—"

Culver lighted a cigarette. He could run a bluff still and Cordo would be uncomfortable, but it would do little good. Pete Cordo had a single-track mind. Culver looked up at the fading stars.

"Okay, Pete," he said quietly, "I'll bring you photographic copies."

HE TURNED on his heel and walked away. He walked confidently but there was a chill wind along his spine. "I've got twenty-four hours to mess this thing out someway," he murmured. "Twenty-four hours—"

It was a very short time for Dean Culver had bluffed and he had not a thing in the world to show Pete Cordo.

He had reached the corner now and he looked back. Cordo's car was breezing away and Black Bart Brunderson was standing on the pavement looking after it. Culver smiled grimly. If he had done nothing else, he had accomplished one thing. With a whisper of suspicion, he had erected a wall between Cordo and Brunderson. His enemies, at least, would not be together. He turned and walked toward his apartment.

Once upon a time, there had been in existence a paper with the signature of Pete Cordo; a paper that would change the map of the underworld if it were published. Pete had signed it when he was a rising young thug and before he had even dreamed of being a big shot. He had signed it in Culver's presence after Dick Dayne, a private dick, had beaten the whey out of him. And in that paper he had ratted on six of his pals. Two of them burned in the chair because of information that Dayne got from that paper, but the confession had never been used as evidence.

Dayne had been killed in an accident but the paper never showed up. Cordo had jumped to the conclusion that Culver had it and he had credited the reporter with enough sense to plant the paper where it would go to the news sheets at his death. And he had been afraid of Culver after he had first got that idea; afraid of him as he was afraid of no one on earth.

Pete Cordo was big but not big enough to stand against evidence that he had once ratted on his pals, that he had committed the unpardonable sin of welching to a bull. He was calling a show-down now because Brunderson had caused him to doubt. He was probably wondering why Culver had never asked money from him. . . .

Culver shook his shoulders as though to shake away the thought of what lay ahead of him. He had no illusions of what would happen to him in twenty-four hours. Pete Cordo would remember all of the years through which he had carried a fear of Culver in his heart and he would not be merciful. He had been known to amuse himself for days with victims who had incurred his personal hate.

Culver turned in at his hotel and made his way to his room. He sighed wearily and dropped on the bed. "Brunderson, Torino and Cordo already," he muttered sleepily, "and the cops maybe, if I stick with Bridwell. Swell opposition. Swell—"

With a grunt, he went off to sleep. He had nerves like that.

CHAPTER FIVE

THREE THIRTY—MOTHER MASON'S

THE JUDGE O'Ryan murder was a press carnival. There were columns of dope, most of it manufactured out of whole cloth; heavily leaded editorials, pages of pictures. The loud cry was raised for Beau Bridwell, but the opposition press had subordinated the subject of the ex-convict and turned the fiercest blasts upon Governor Barker. Why had he defied the parole board and released a man sworn to kill Judge O'Ryan? Did the Judge's investigation of the

It was a snatch in the best gangland fashion. Pete Cordo's men had struck again.

governor's appointments and the promised revelations in the wake of the investigation have anything to do with that strange pardon? The opposition press wanted to know.

The administration papers were defending the governor valiantly with very little to go on. They pointed out that Judge O'Ryan was the governor's life-long friend and that there was no evidence to support the idea that the Judge's investigation would involve the governor in anything discreditable. They did not try to explain the Bridwell pardon but they skirted it by pointing to the fact that it was a personal phone call of the governor's which had resulted in discovery of the murder.

All of the papers were up in the air about the identity of the man who answered the phone in Judge O'Ryan's residence. Culver grinned, flipped the papers aside and went to call on Beau Bridwell.

Bridwell was pathetically glad to see him. His hideout was a narrow room partitioned off in the basement of Mother Mason's. It was a grimy, dingy, damp and uncomfortable hole but it was practically police-proof and some distinguished fugitives had found it a haven. The little crook literally pawed him for news. Culver looked at him.

"They're after you hot," he said bluntly. "But tell me something. Are you tied up with any of the mobs?"

Bridwell's eyes widened. "No. I steered away from everybody till I came to you. I was away nine years, you know, and—"

"You didn't recognize any of those bozos at O'Ryan's?"

"Nope. Didn't even see 'em clear. It was dark and they had their backs turned when they got near the lantern."

Culver's eyes were suspicious. "The safe didn't look like it had been touched."

"No?" Bridwell seemed genuinely startled. They were in front of it when I lammed out. Unless—" He frowned.

"Unless what?"

"Somebody might have been able to open it by the feel. You know—Listen to the tumblers." He shook his head sadly. "There never were many that could do it and I guess maybe there's less now."

"Could you open a safe like that?"

Fear shadowed Bridwell's eyes for a moment. He gulped a little, nodded. "Yes. Even big boxes and trick construction stuff like the Judge's." Pride banished the fear as he spoke and he seemed like another person altogether. Culver shot a question abruptly.

"Bridwell, did you kill O'Ryan?"

The little crook jumped, threw a terrified glance at the door. No. No. I swear I didn't."

"Well, you're holding back something. Come clean!"

"No. No. I swear. I told you the whole story, Culver—"

THERE WAS deadly fear in Bridwell's face, the fear of a man whose fate lies in the hands of another. Culver could destroy him with a word and he knew no reason why Culver should protect him if it came to a jam.

Culver's eyes were still probing the washed out little man's face. Something eluded him. The man was honest in his answers and yet there was something still to be explained, some angle that Bridwell touched or controlled and of which he refused to speak. Culver did not believe that Bridwell had killed the judge nor that he knew the murderers, but he knew something. Yet with his very life at stake now, if he wouldn't divulge his knowledge to the only ally he had, there was some factor in the case that Culver would have to unearth for himself.

He was on the verge of challenging point-blank on the point of Bridwell's escape from an upstairs window when the way to the downstairs window was open. He checked the impulse, however, as a sudden flash of inspiration came to him. There was a question that he had forgotten to put to Bridwell; a perfectly straight question and one that hit straight at the heart of the O'Ryan murder. It was so obvious that he had glossed right over it and yet the O'Ryan killing could not be explained nor solved until that question was answered. And Bridwell, he felt, held the key.

There was an exultant gleam in Dean Culver's eyes and if the threat of living only twenty four hours had not been hanging over him, he would have forced an answer to his question from Beau Bridwell on the moment and saved himself an uncomfortable train ride. As it was, he merely laughed tolerantly.

"Stick it out, Kid," he said. "I'll be dropping in later."

He was still smiling when he left Mother Mason's but the smile froze on his lips as he started down the steps toward his own car. Directly across the street there was a long racy touring car with the side curtains up. Such cars had a sinister significance now. Culver's eyes narrowed. He could feel fingers of ice moving along his spine but he knew that there was no advantage in retreat. He moved steadily down the steps.

Cordo's twenty four hours weren't up but there was always the chance that Vito Torino would get brave and bull the show; especially now when his patron, Bart Brunderson, had failed in an attempt to deal with Pete Cordo.

Culver's feet touched the pavement and nothing happened. He stood for a few seconds looking at his own car and calmly lighted a cigarette. Still nothing happened and he turned casually and walked across the street to the dark car.

THERE WAS only one man in it; a man as old as Bridwell whose face was coarse and puffy and whose eyes were, for the moment, fish-like, although Culver had seen them different. There was a silly, uncertain smile on the man's face and he gripped the wheel tight. The engine was turning over. Culver nodded.

"How are you, Dick. Waiting for someone?"

The man looked doubtful, at a loss for words; as though things were not happening as he expected. "Yeah," he said. Culver grinned. He knew Dick Harper of old and it was one of the minor mysteries of the big town how the brain scrambled old timer held his place in a young and coming mob like Vito Torino's. A booze fighter who had once been something in the world of crime, Dick Harper had been down to the extremity of rolling drunks in gutters and begging dimes along the big stem when prohibition came in. Now he had money and a job in a good mob and no more intelligence than a baby monkey with which to justify what he got. He wasn't even tough. His fellow mobsters took most of his money away from him when he got a split and nothing was ever done about it.

Culver was no wiser than anybody else and Harper had never interested him enough to prompt investigation. Today, however, he was glad that Dick Harper was a member of the Torino mob and that fate had delivered him into his hands. He smiled disarmingly.

"You wouldn't kid me, Dick," he said. "You were waiting out here because Vito saw me go into Mother Mason's and got curious. He figured that if he left this big bump wagon out here, I'd be plenty scared and hop right into my wagon and streak. Your job was to follow me and find out where I went. Right?"

Harper was staring dazedly and Culver chuckled. "You're a pretty swell hack herder they tell me."

Dick Harper's drink dulled features lighted for a minute. "I'm the best that Vito's got," he said.

Culver knew differently, but he let it ride. When he got a sucker patting himself on the back, he kept him patting till his arm got tired. He was already shaping Dick Harper into his plans.

"Dick," he said soberly, "that's just the point. You're not only the best hack herder in the outfit; the only man they could trust to follow me on a getaway, but you're an old timer. You played the game when Vito wore diapers. You ought to be the brains of the gang."

Dick Harper's dead eyes came momentarily to life. He glowed for a second and then went as cold as a discarded cigar butt. "They don't trust me," he said bitterly. "Figure I'm too old."

"That's where they're foolish, Dick. Keeping you on small stuff."

Harper stiffened. "I don't just do small stuff," he said defensively. "You were talkin' about bein' the brains. I do big stuff. I—"

HIS THIN jaws snapped shut. Dean Culver's eyes narrowed, but he didn't press the point. "I'm going to give you a break, Dick," he said, "to show you I'm on the level with you. I'll tell you where I'm going. I'm going to go down to the station and buy a ticket to Castleton. I've got a girl out there and I'm going to lay low. Cordo is a bit off me and I want to give him chance to cool off."

He was watching the old timer narrowly and he saw that the Cordo information was not news. Harper knew about it and it scored by convincing him of Culver's truthfulness. There was a suspicious look in the bloated face, however, and Culver played to that look.

"You can follow me along and check up, Dick," he said. "I expect you to. You're smart and I know you don't believe anybody till you're shown. That's right."

Harper glowed again and his guard was down. Culver leaned closer. "Now I'll give you a real tip. Be back here about three thirty tomorrow A. M. and watch the door of Mother Mason's. You'll see something, Dick, that will make Vito and all the rest of those young squirts take their hats off to you when you tell them."

Dick Harper wet his lips and Culver saw that he was hooked. "Is that the goods?" he whispered huskily. Culver laughed.

"I am not getting paid for lying to you am I? I don't stand to win anything, do I?"

He stepped back before Harper had time to ask any further questions and he heard the man mutter. "I'll be here, Culver. Thanks."

He laughed and walked across to his own car. There was nothing in Dean Culver's code of ethics that made it a crime to kid a bum like Dick Harper. There was no slinking, murderous gangster job that Harper wouldn't lend himself to, and, despite that muttered

"Thanks," he'd sink a knife in Culver's back tomorrow for a bottle of cheap hooch.

With the dark car following him, Culver drove straight to the station, parked his car and bought a ticket to Capital City. He was not worried about the possibility of Harper checking his ticket buy. A sloppy yegg of the Harper stamp would take his destination as Castleton for granted as long as he fulfilled the easily checked up part of his statement and drove directly to the station.

"There's some good reason for having Harper in that mob," Culver said thoughtfully as he entered the train shed, "but it's one helluva mistake to use him for anything but the reason that makes him valuable whatever the reason is. Vito Torino tries to get his money's worth and this is one time when he gets more than he bargained for."

His brain was already busy at the weaving of a web that would catch a choice bunch of flies when the clock in Mother Mason's banged three thirty.

CHAPTER SIX

THE LITTLE BLACK BOOK

THE PRESS had been unable to reach the governor for an interview. He was not at the executive mansion, and his secretaries professed ignorance. Dean Culver didn't let that worry him. He had a little black book in which he had made jottings over a long period of years on the papers. There was quite a little about Governor Barker.

Under the heading of "Friends" there appeared the name of Dennis Slattery. To Culver, the item was a tip-off. Slattery owned the Parkway-Plaza in Capital City. It was a swell spot for a governor to lie low incognito. Under the heading of "Peculiarities" there was another significant item on the Governor. "Smokes Russian cigarettes in preference to cigars."

A small item! And it had been a dreary job assembling such trivia about hundreds of men in the public eye. Occasionally though, as now, the book paid big dividends. The first thing that Culver did at the end of the three-hour train ride to the Capital was to buy a package of Russian cigarettes at an exclusive cigar store. The second thing that he did was to empty the cigarettes into a refuse can. He kept the package and went to the Parkway Plaza, where he registered under his own name.

He was back down in the lobby five minutes after being shown to his room. He eased up to the cigar stand like a nervous man who is timid about making known his wants.

"I don't suppose you have what I want," he said hesitantly. "I generally carry a supply but they are hard to get. . . ." His voice trailed off and he fumbled the empty cigarette case out of his pocket.

The cigar clerk frowned as he tried to follow the vague and hesitant preamble; then he squinted at the package and smiled.

"Ah, Russians! Well, you're in luck, my friend. We don't usually carry them. No call for them generally; but a gentleman up in 702 wanted them and I laid in a few. Glad now I did."

Culver was conventionally

pleased as he bought his package of Russians. Inside he was laughing silently. He had succeeded easier than he had hoped. The best that he had anticipated was that the unusual request presented in an apologetic manner would lead the man to make some comment that would give Culver a clue to follow up; maybe by way of the Bell Captain. A governor in retreat, of course, would not buy cigarettes himself; he would send down for them. Culver turned away.

"Room 702," he said softly. "Well, now for a plan of the hotel and I'm set."

A distant, unseen clock was chiming eleven when he walked down the quiet hall of the seventh floor and stepped out on the fire escape nearest to the governor's suite.

The lighted battle monument two squares away looked unreal. The street below was a residence street and it was quiet, indifferently lighted and exceedingly remote. Down the sheer face of the hotel, there was shadow; sliced in two or three places by the yellow gleam from the lighted rooms within. Culver looked at the narrow coping that he must walk to the Governor's suite and shivered. He was no acrobat, and he would have preferred dangers with which he was more familiar, but there was no alternative. He shook his shoulders impatiently and stepped out.

SEVEN stories of empty space yawned under him. The blare of a taxi almost rocked him from his perch. His toes and fingers cramped and the sweat beaded on his forehead; then the darkened window that was his goal loomed ahead of him. He rested his palms on the sill and tried to forget the yawning space behind him. With appreciation, he noted that the window was part way open for ventilation. Balancing carefully, he widened the aperture, slid his foot over the sill and stepped into the velvet darkness of 702.

As was to be expected, 702 was a suite. Culver found himself in the parlor, and he was grateful for the breathing space. Carefully he wiped his hands in a handkerchief and worked the stiffness out of his fingers. He felt the automatic in his shoulder holster and eased the tiny flashlight from his hip. Moving softly, he crossed the floor to the connecting door which was open and stepped into the bed room. Heavy breathing guided him to the bed.

He stood there for a second, and then pressed the button of his flashlight and sent a stabbing beam of light into the face of the man on the bed.

The lean, well moulded features of Governor Franklin Barker were revealed in the spot of light, and Culver gave an inward grunt of satisfaction. There was always the outside chance that he had made a mistake. As the beam of light hit him, the governor shuddered and blinked his eyes open. Startled, he half raised himself in the bed.

"What's—what's the matter?" he gasped. "Who. . . ."

"Take it easy, governor. No loud chatter. Nothing's going to happen to you." Culver's voice was hard, commanding. The governor, fully awake now, stared into the light as though trying to see beyond it. He was remarkably self-possessed for a man awakened so abruptly.

"Suppose we have a little more light so we can both see," he said. His hand came up slowly to the reading light above his bed, but his movements were deliberate and he waited for permission. Culver nodded.

"Okay if you watch your step. Might as well be comfortable."

The reading light came on and Culver pocketed his flash. The eyes of the two men met. Culver had his automatic in his hand. He moved it slightly and his voice was almost apologetic.

"If you tell me that I don't need this thing for self protection and give me your word on it," he said, "I'll put it away."

The governor smiled. "I'm curious and that's your guarantee," he said. "I'll give you my word, if that's all you want, that I won't take any measures except in self defense."

"Okay." Culver pocketed the automatic and stretched his legs. "This is the only way I could get an interview with you. I'm the guy that talked to you over the phone the other night."

The governor stiffened and his face paled perceptibly. Culver read the thought that passed through his mind and gestured impatiently. "Judge O'Ryan was dead when I got there," he said. "That's why I want to talk to you. I didn't have anything to do with it and I don't think that Bridwell did."

Franklin Barker relaxed. "You're not Bridwell, then. Mind if I smoke?"

He looked around him and Culver dipped into his pocket. "No, I'm not Bridwell, but I know where he is. I've got some of your favorite brand here. Take 'em."

THE GOVERNOR looked more bewildered than ever as he accepted the proffered package of Russians. "This is an extraordinary experience," he said slowly. "If neither one of us is crazy, it makes it even more extraordinary."

Culver was measuring the man through narrowed eyelids and he liked what he saw. Franklin Barker had courage and intelligence. He had undoubtedly been a tool of the political machine, but, if he had, it was because there was no other way of gaining the heights in the career he had chosen. No man became governor unless he pleased the politicians, but Culver was beginning to understand the pressure which had led to the O'Ryan investigation. Barker, once he was in power, would be a hard man for the ring to control. They had to trick him.

"If anyone is crazy," he said, "I'm it. Before I ask you for anything, governor, I'm going to trust you with a long spiel that's got personal and confidential written all over it."

The governor was looking at him curiously. "Thank you," he said.

Weighing his words carefully, Culver plunged into the account of his activities on the night that O'Ryan was killed. He related Bridwell's story, the appearance of the room and the subsequent events at Big John Zoro's. The governor listened gravely and Culver applauded him silently for the way in which he masked his emotions. Here was a poker player.

"There's the deal to date," he concluded, "and you can play with the police if you want to. I can't stop you once I leave here. But the police in the big town take orders from a lot of people who might not be your friends. I'm willing to be on your side because I can do myself more good that way."

The governor smiled. "Frank enough. What do you want?"

Culver's face was grim. "This thing means your official life," he said bluntly. "It means the only life I've got. I can do you an awful lot of good and you can do more than a little for me if you come clean. Why did you give Bridwell a rain check?"

"'Rain check?' Oh, you mean that pardon." The governor frowned thoughtfully. "You can't quote me because you never saw me officially. I can prove that nobody has talked to me." He lighted a cigarette. "I pardoned Bridwell because Lee Hodgson told me that the parole board was voting the recommendation. He called me up and said that he was anxious to expedite matters because Bridwell's mother was dying and that, out of sympathy, some fellow crooks of his had placed evidence in Bart Brunderson's hands that proved Bridwell to be innocent of the crime he was expiating."

Culver stared incredulously. "You fell for that?"

The governor shook his head. "I appointed Hodgson, but I wasn't that careless in an election year. I called Bart Brunderson."

CULVER straightened. His eyes were gleaming as he leaned forward. "So Brunderson isn't trying to elect you? That bothered me. Go on. They both denied later that they had ever mentioned Bridwell to you, of course."

The governor nodded. "Certainly. That's the first time that I knew that Brunderson wasn't behind me. O'Ryan warned me, but I guess the best of us make mistakes. . . ."

Culver was frowning now. "You're the state ticket of Brunderson's party," he said. "What's he throwing the party for in a national election year? He backed you at the convention that re-nominated you."

The governor's eyes were half closed. "He did back me at the convention. That threw me off the track. Does it mean anything to you that our party has control of the Big Town with no election for a year there, and that our party is practically certain to elect the national ticket this year? That if I went over for another term, our party would control every bit of political nourishment in the state practically; national, state and municipal?"

Dean Culver sat silent with his eyes on the governor's face. Suddenly he clenched his fist. His eyes lighted with unholy joy. "I get it!" he said. "I've been blind as a bat. The other party's been in control of Federal money for years, and the bosses have traded favors with Bart Brunderson. He doesn't want them washed out of this state because there might be a new gang if they ever got back in power, and he'd be in the cold."

The governor grinned appreciatively. "That's it exactly." His face hardened. "He's willing to throw the state and ruin me to let the opposition put their candidate over and keep a place open at the public trough. He'll have enough graft with Federal patronage to dispense and with his strange hold on the big town." His jaw hardened. "He hasn't had any too rich pickings up state anyway."

Culver relaxed in his chair. The whole story was unreeling in his brain like a moving picture on a screen. It was not Franklin Barker who was menaced by the O'Ryan investigation, although the investigation had been forced as a frame for the governor. O'Ryan had warned Barker. That meant that he had stumbled across something that gave him a clue to what Brunderson was trying to do. He had tried to warn the governor, but he probably hadn't had enough to back up his advice—or he was waiting for more data to develop.

"Why did you call O'Ryan in the middle of the night?" Culver's voice was sharp. The governor's eyes clouded.

"I was working on a speech when I came to the conclusion that we've reached tonight. It came to me suddenly that the Judge's life was in danger if it occurred to anybody that he might be a menace to the little grab that was being planned."

CULVER nodded. "A lot of men have been blotted for less than the 'take' that Brunderson's gang gets every year. Well, governor, I'm much obliged, and you won't be sorry you talked."

He rose to his feet and the governor eyed him speculatively. "You don't think Brunderson killed him?"

"No. I don't. There's no reason why he should do any dirty work."

"Well," the governor's eyes clouded, "I don't see what particular good this talk did you. What I've been telling you is not evidence, you know. No court would admit the statements I have made nor the conclusions you've drawn. Why, even the newspapers would laugh. As for the public? Well, you know what the man in the street would say about my story of this affair."

Culver nodded. "I know. It's because there is so much mileage between fact and evidence that things have to be done the way I do them. The public wouldn't understand me, either."

"But what do you propose to do? What can you do?"

Culver's face was grim. "I'll ask a question first. The District Attorney down in the big town is an awful pain in the neck to Brunderson and his crowd. I think he's a damned pussy footer myself, but he's got guts enough to buck the machine. Can you do anything with him?"

The governor frowned thoughtfully. "I might if I could convince him that Brunderson crossed me and that I'm not trying to frame him. I'd have to know what you wanted, though. I don't want to make a deal with him unless I have to. . . ."

"Well, if you can do it and you're gambler enough, tell him I'm going to be in touch with him and that I'm shooting square—for him to do just what I tell him to do even if it looks like political suicide."

"I am afraid that will be hard to do."

"I know it," Culver walked toward the door and stopped. "You're a gone duck in this state unless you can do it," he said crisply, "and it's only a matter of time till that D. A. is framed nicely, too. Think that over."

"And if I can do it?"

"Well, in that case—and provided that I can keep Pete Cordo

from rubbing me out—I'll smash Bart Brunderson so wide open that he'll never bother you again.''

The governor sighed. ''I wish I could believe you,'' he said. ''But, believing or not, it's worth the gamble. I'll see what I can do with Mr. Joyce.''

CHAPTER SEVEN

DEATH RIDE

IT LACKED a couple of minutes of three A. M. when Culver left the upstate train at the Big Town terminal. There was a telephone booth in a corner of the big station and he made for it. The number that he spoke into the mouthpiece was a number used by a very few people; the private number of Pete Cordo. For a few seconds he waited and then a sleepy voice growled into the transmitter and Culver grinned. In a voice deliberately thickened he growled back.

''Cordo? Well, never mind who this is. I got dope for you. How'd you like to have the papers that O'Ryan was killed for?''

He felt the tension at the other end of the line. Pete Cordo was taking a few seconds for the question to sink in; then he swore.

''What you do? Kid me? Who's 'is?''

''Cut the fool questions. I'm telling you enough. Beau Bridwell is hiding out in Mother Mason's downstairs room. You know about that room, don't you? He has the papers ditched some place and Culver is making a deal to sell 'em to Brunderson. Torino's mob is going to protect Culver from you if the deal goes through. Get that?''

Culver grinned again as he heard Pete Cordo curse in thick gutturals. Nothing could be better calculated to wake him up than that crack about Torino protecting anybody that he wanted to get. Cordo was growling into the receiver again.

''How do I know this is not a kid? Who is 'is?''

''I'd be crazy to tell you who this is, but you can check up on the rest. There's one of Torino's men watching Mother Mason's in case Bridwell decides to blow. Better pick him up. You'll tip your hand if you burn him down. Those papers are worth a million to you, Cordo.''

''But why you give me something like that? What the hell? This is one big kid. Who is 'is?''

''Aw to hell with you, you dumb ape. Stay in bed if you don't want it.''

Culver clicked the receiver. He was grinning broadly now. There wasn't a chance in the world of Pete Cordo staying in bed. He might be doubtful but he'd check up. Once he found that the salient features of the story clicked, he'd be in for everything he had.

''I didn't kid him much at that.''

Culver sobered as he faced the gamble that he would have to take himself. He was in control so far but any one of a number of little things could turn the tables on him fast now—and he was playing this hand with blue chips. His life was on the table and he had cards to draw.

He retrieved his car which was parked near the station and drove to within a block of Mother Mason's. Hugging the shadows, he traversed the rest of the way on foot. The neighborhood was badly lighted and that helped. He entered the alley on the corner below his objective and came up the alley until he was behind the rooming house; then he slipped between two houses and traversed an areaway to where he had a good view of the street.

THERE WAS a man loitering in the shadows across the way and Culver gave a grunt of satisfaction. Dick Harper was on the job. He'd been a little leery of Harper but the man had taken the bait hard. The stage was set for Cordo.

The first intimation of the great one's coming was a second shadow that slipped out a dark slit between the shabby old houses across the street. Dick Harper, unsuspecting and slow-witted, was not aware of that shadow for several seconds after Culver first discerned it. Then it was too late. Something rose and fell swiftly and Harper slumped. The other man caught him just as a big car swept around the corner.

With a faint rustle of tires against the curb, the big car came to a stop. For seconds nothing happened. Cordo was cautious of traps. One of his body-guards, a squat gorilla-like shape in the dim streets, slid out of the tonneau and looked carefully up and down the street. There was a low whistle from across the way and the look-out turned. Culver recognized him as Hymie Katz, a lightning fast man with the gun and notorious as the killer of Bump Edwards; the killing that had made Pete Cordo the czar of the underworld.

Walking with a rolling swagger, Katz was crossing the street. In a few seconds he came back with the man who had laid Dick Harper low. They were carrying the slumped form of the Torino gangster and without any waste motion, they dumped it in the back of the car. Nothing alarming had happened and Pete Cordo got out, a hulking giant who towered above his henchmen. Culver sank deeper into the shadows as the three opened the rusty gate and started quietly along the flagged walk toward the back of Mother Mason's. He had them all tagged now; Cordo, Katz and Monty Morello. There was only one more factor to reckon with; the driver of the car. That undoubtedly would be Bill Gregory who was the ghost of a dream gone wrong. Gregory had once bossed Kerry Patch and had had ambitions; now he was Cordo's star driver and glad to be alive.

Culver's car was not far away and he had a chance of following this crowd if he had to, but it would be a risky play. This was no collection of ham talent. They would spot a trailer in a very few minutes and that might be sorrowful. Culver also had a gun and a good chance of sticking up Bill Gregory. He was about Gregory's build and he might get away with taking the fellow's place. He was very doubtful, though, about getting accurate dope from Gregory on where he was to drive; even with a gun as persuader. He'd be in a very bad spot if he drove to the wrong place.

A slight scraping noise sounded along the stone flags that ran around Mother Mason's. A second or two later, three men emerged into the semi-gloom of the badly lighted street. Cordo walked alone but the other two dragged another man between them; a struggling mite of humanity who had been roughly gagged and partially trussed up—Beau Bridwell.

The driver was leaning out of the car. Cordo, with a quick glance up and down the street, snapped his fingers. The driver's head disappeared and the two men swung their burden swiftly into the back of the car. Cordo stepped over the squirming body and Hymie Katz swung in beside him. Monty Morello was getting in beside the driver. Katz reached out to slam the door and Gregory ran the engine up.

AT THAT moment, Culver came out of hiding like a leopard on the leap for game. He had shed his shoes and he moved close to the ground with a terrific burst of speed. The door slammed and the engine roared. Culver leaped for the split type rear bumper, locked his arm in the spare tire and hung on. The car leaped away and he could feel the wrench in his shoulder sockets until he established his balance and swayed with the motion of the big eight. He was hanging almost straight out as they whisked around a corner, then he bumped back and the car levelled out . . .

Twisted pretzel-like on his insecure perch, Culver was not visible from inside the car. There was always a chance that a policeman or a late prowling nitwit of a pedestrian would call attention to him, but he discounted that risk as negligible. The hour was late and Cordo was not likely to drive along the brightly lighted boulevards with two prisoners on the floor at his feet.

Swinging off the smooth macadam without warning the car jounced for three blocks over a mad causeway of cobblestones. Culver gritted his teeth. "It's better than the kind of a ride that Cordo would like to take me on." The sentence bounced in his brain; then the car roared off on a fairly straight street that had paving of a sort, slithered around a corner and straightened out. Culver forgot his discomfort. The route could only lead to one spot on the Cordo map.

"The cider mill!" he muttered. His eyes lighted with satisfaction.

Several miles beyond the city limits and located in a deep depression between two embryo hills, the cider mill had once been an integral part of the crude system adopted for the making of liquor in the early days of prohibition. Secrecy had been necessary in those days and no one could approach the old mill in a car without advertising himself well in advance, nor could a sufficient number of men constitute a raiding party or stage a surprise attack. Since the liquor business had come out in the open, there had been little need for the cider mill, but the underworld knew that a couple of the Cordo "rides" had ended up there and that Pete Cordo still used the ramshackle group of buildings for purposes of his own.

They were rolling now over a country road; narrow and rutted. Culver could not look ahead of the car but he tensed for the moment when they reached the turn-off. The car jolted and there was a growl as the driver shifted gears. Culver let go, rolled over and pulled his body flat at the side of the road. He saw the tail light of the car lift and then bob away as the big car turned off and started down the

"Sorry for the intrusion," droned Culver. "But move a muscle, Senator, and you are a dead man."

rough tortuous road that led to the Cider Mill. He spat a mouthful of gravel and smiled grimly. He'd gotten away with the big risk and he had nearly a mile to walk and then—

He left future events to the future and started down the road in the wake of the car; a scarcely perceptible humming sound now in the distance.

CHAPTER EIGHT

AT THE CIDER MILL

A SCATTERED pile of crumbling stone ruins beside a dry stream bed; that was the Cider Mill. A group of mound like hills surrounded it. To the right of the mill proper was a blackened area of charred ground where a house had once stood, behind it and to the left the trees grew thickly. Laced through the trees and hung in double layers from deeply imbedded posts in front of the old stone pile was the barbed wire.

Dean Culver crawled through the wire above the blackened area and noted with satisfaction that there was a light showing on the main floor of the old dive. No curtain, shutter or shade dimmed that light and that simplified his problem. After all, why should Cordo be careful out here at four in the morning?

A few minutes of cautious movement brought Culver within range of that window. Nothing else seemed to move in all creation. The car loomed black and deserted some twenty-five yards away. A hum of voices came from the direction of the window. Pressed against the damp wall, Culver edged toward the lighted square. He could hear the voices now; rather, he could hear Pete Cordo's heavy guttural voice.

"Come through, yuh mutt! We know you got them papers o' O'Ryan's."

Bridwell's thin, frightened voice carried well. "No. No. It was all a frame, I tell you. I don't know anything."

There was a tense silence; then Cordo's voice again. "Got them things hot?"

Culver's lips were tight against his teeth. His fate was riding on a few words now; his whole scheme, perhaps his life. He risked a look through the window.

Hymie Katz, with a vicious look of anticipation on his face was turning from the fireplace with an ice tong in his hands. The tips of the tongs glowed red. Across the room sat Pete Cordo, a cigarette hanging on his loose lower lip, his eyes squinted malevolently in the direction of Beau Bridwell. The shabby little convict lay on the stone flooring, his hands and feet securely tied, a look of wild terror in his faded eyes. Hymie Katz started across the floor toward him. Pete Cordo waved his hand.

"Stick one 'o them prongs in each of his ears. If he won't talk, he won't listen neither . . ."

Culver's nerves were taut. He eased the gun in his shoulder holster and wet his lips. Bridwell was wiggling frantically as though he would crawl away from the fate that was bearing down upon him. Suddenly he screamed.

"Keep it away. Keep it away. I'll tell you. I'll tell you!"

Pete Cordo's hand went up. He leaned forward and spat toward the terrified man on the floor. "Chirp quick!"

Bridwell was strangling with terror. "I took the papers," he moaned. "I got them. I cleaned the box before those other guys got there. But I didn't croak the judge. I swear I didn't croak the judge. I . . ."

"The hell with the judge. Where's the papers?" Cordo was breathing heavily. Bridwell looked at him wide eyed. Culver was quivering. This was what he wanted. He'd suspected that Bridwell had those papers the last time he talked to him. He'd let him run to get two birds with a single shot.

"The papers are out at O'Ryan's, in a little tool house. There was a lot of them. I ditched 'em after the other guys croaked the judge. I could take you to 'em. They're safe there . . ."

CORDO was squinting at Bridwell with a look of cold malevolence. "That better be straight," he growled, "or getting hot pincers in your ears will just be play to what you'll get . . ."

Culver relaxed and hugged the wall beside the window. Cordo was growling again. "What did you want the papers for, you mugg?"

"I don't know. I don't know." Bridwell was obviously blown up. "I figured that pardon I got was screwy. I thought I'd have something to make a deal with if they tried to run me back. I . . ."

Something hard jabbed Culver in the spine. A low pitched voice sounded in his ear. "Steady, Bucko, and step back here. Keep your hands up!"

The world was crashing about Culver's ears and he cursed himself inwardly for taking anything for granted, for becoming absorbed in the conversation within and dropping his guard. An expert hand moved over his body while the gun held hard against his back. He felt his own gun slipped from its holster but he didn't dare make a play. A man who has his back to an armed foe is outmanouvered before he starts.

"All right. Now turn around and give me a look at you!"

Culver turned slowly and cursed softly. The man who had captured him was Bill Gregory. He might have figured that they'd leave the driver outside for a lookout. Gregory was grinning at him. A gesture commanded him away from the vicinity of the window. Gregory was having his minute and he proposed to enjoy it.

"So, it's smart-boy Culver?" he sneered. "Welcome to our city. Seems like somebody told me you were too bright for the dumb boys in the racket. Right?"

"I didn't say so, did I?"

"You got caught like a dumb flatfoot." There was a spiteful look of triumph on the gangster's face. "At that, I'm sorry for you. What you'll get when I bring you in will be huge."

He leaned forward. "I'd tell you to jump my gun and take it clean instead o' goin' in only I wouldn't kill you. I'd just drop you. The boss wouldn't forgive me if I spoiled his fun."

Culver's eyes were level, his face expressionless. "Seems as though I remember you being a boss one time?" he said slowly. "The place was Kerry Patch or something like that, wasn't it."

Gregory's eyes smouldered. "Never you mind that. I'm smarter than a lot of bosses in this town. What I started to tell you was what was going to happen to you." He stuck his jaw out. "Maybe you remember Matty Coyne. The boss pulled all o' his nice red hair out in little bunches with a pliers. He was bald headed when he got the rest. Want me to tell you the rest?"

"Never mind, Bill. Mind if I take a smoke before you take me in?" Culver seemed suddenly to slump. The spirit went out of him. Bill Gregory grinned.

"Go ahead, but don't forget this gun, guy."

"I won't." Culver fished out a limp package and offered a smoke to his captor. Bill Gregory declined with a sly smile to reach for the package. Holding the gun steady, he brought forth a smoke from his own pocket. He was not worrying about weapons. He had frisked Culver carefully. Nor did Culver seem to be thinking of weapons. He was a slumped, dejected figure. Taking a cigar lighter from his vest pocket, he held it out.

INSTINCTIVELY, Gregory leaned forward; then he started to draw back. He wasn't fast enough. There was a hissing sputter and a sharp report like the cracking of a dry twig. Bill Gregory gasped and reeled back on his heels. The gun roared.

Culver side-stepped like a fighter at the moment that he pressed the tear gas cartridge release on the lighter. With a pantherish leap he closed in to the left of the roaring gun. His right fist dropped and came up like a rocket. As it exploded against the gangster's jaw, he swept over with his left hand and wrenched the gun free. Blinded with gas and numbed by the blow, Bill Gregory plunged forward and fell face down on the ground.

Sounds of hurried movement came from the Mill. A man stood stupidly framed in the lighted window for a fraction of a second with a gun in his hand and Culver fired. The light went out and there was a whistling gasp from beyond the window. Culver faded out close to the ground. His lips tightened back over his teeth.

"Exit Monty Morello!" He muttered. "Next!"

The echo of his shot died and a smothering silence fell over the Cider Mill. Culver pressed his body close to the ground and waited. He heard a careful movement to his right, and his hand tightened on the trigger. Bill Gregory was climbing groggily to his feet.

Pawing at his eyes and rocking back on his heels like a punch drunk pug, the gangster started to weave his unsteady way toward the doorway of the mill. Culver crawled quietly after him. Bill Gregory quite evidently was in a muddled frame of mind. He did not quite know what had happened to him, but there was some instinct operative in his mind that was urging him to seek the sanctuary of the mill. Culver sensed drama in that decision.

"Maybe he knows now why he isn't a big shot," he whispered. "Too much mouth. If he'd taken me in, instead of hanging around and making a damned barber out of himself, he'd have been a hero...."

Bill Gregory was facing the door now. He fumbled in his pocket for Culver's automatic, drew it and started up the steps. Culver's eyes narrowed and he held his own weapon ready. "Cordo will figure that, since there was only one shot the first time and a damned hostile shot the next time, that anybody left out here is the enemy...."

Bill Gregory had reached the top step. He swayed there and his foot scraped the stone. The door opened with hair raising suddenness and flame stabbed the darkness. There was a sharp report and Gregory stiffened to his full height. The man in the doorway fired again. As Gregory broke in two and slumped forward with his hands against his middle, Culver laid a bullet straight through the doorway.

He heard a strangled cry, the surprised, hurt cry of a man who considers himself victor only to find defeat and death reaching for him. The gun in the doorway spoke again and the flash came low, the bullet going off wild into the trees. The location of that flash told much. The man who was firing was falling as he fired.

Culver blazed another bullet across sill-high and shifted his position. The echoes boomed weirdly through the mill and tumbled off into silence. Culver wet his lips.

"That would be Hymie Katz! Cordo coming up...."

HE COULD not afford to make any mistakes now. Pete Cordo was plenty bad with the gun. He did not take part in gun battles while he had hired men handy, but he had held his own when he was coming up and he would be a dangerous article when cornered. As long as he holed up in that old stone fort, he'd be safe from a lone aggressor moving about in the darkness.

Culver frowned and then shrugged. "I'll take a chance that he won't dare shoot at a voice and that he wouldn't hit me if he did shoot at my voice."

Shifting toward the trees and the parked car, Culver sent a shout toward the Mill. "All right, you Cordo! Stay there. I'll be back with the boys. . . ."

His shout woke more echoes but there was no reply from the Mill. Culver moved swiftly to the far side of the parked car. The keys were in the ignition and he set the switch. Then he sprawled along the running board and reached in until he could press the starter with his hand. The engine burst into song, full throated and roaring. Almost at the same instant, there came a flash and a roar from the wing of the house closest to the car—then another and another and another.

It was good shooting and it riddled the spot where Culver would have been if he'd tried to drive the car away. Inflating his lungs, Culver gave a wild scream and, reaching into the car, pulled the throttle open wide. The fierce roar of a big eight turned full gun and racing shook the very trees. Culver smiled grimly and rolled off behind the car, crawling rapidly toward the mill once more.

To anybody willing to accept the evidence of his senses, it would appear that one of those viciously pumped bullets had killed the man in the car, and that he had fallen on the throttle. There was something horribly convincing about that roaring engine, something nerve destroying. Culver had to fight the insane impulse to go and turn the thing off himself. He did not think that Cordo could resist it.

Cordo didn't. He waited for a horrible three minutes of roaring sound and then he crept slowly from the mill, his gun in his hand. Culver recognized the unmistakable outline of that hulking form and his lips curled.

"The big shot himself—doing his thinking in person. If he had a brain, he'd turn Bridwell loose and make him investigate."

Carefully he stalked the crouching figure of the big gangster. The man was within ten paces of the car, when Culver materialized out of the shadows at his back. He had to shout to make his voice carry over the roar of horse-power rampant.

"Game's up, Cordo! Hoist 'em."

Pete Cordo bent at the knees and stiffened. He might have been a man straining to hear, a rabbit frightened half to death and hesitating on the verge of flight. Or a mad killer who hears the unwelcome sound of taps. For a second, he stood thus and then he whirled with tigerish speed, his gun coming up with flame coloring the muzzle.

HIS LIPS a thin line and his features frozen granite hard, Dean Culver stood with his feet firmly planted, waited a split second till his man had whirled completely around and then squeezed the trigger. He only fired once, but Pete Cordo's long arms were flung wildly as he completed his desperate spin, his gun fell from his hand as he collapsed. One shot had been plenty.

Dean Culver smiled a hard smile, and slowly removed his hat. He looked quizzically at the neat hole that had been drilled in his head covering and ran his hand thoughtfully through his hair. He turned the body of Pete Cordo over and exposed the wide, reddening stain on the man's chest.

"Anyway, Pete," he said quietly, "I didn't get you in the back. You went out pouring it. . . ."

He turned soberly toward the house, suddenly conscious of an overwhelming sense of weariness. The past hour had been a terrific strain and killing depressed him, although he was not squeamish about gangsters. Since mobsters were so adept at giving it, it was his philosophy that they should expect to take it.

Still there was something about snuffing a man that produced a wave of brain nausea. One didn't like to think of it too much.

Hymie Katz lay sprawled in the little hallway inside the door. Hymie was quite dead, and Culver did not go into any detailed examination beyond that. He switched on the light. Beau Bridwell looked up at him with wide eyes.

"Where—how did you get here, Culver?"

Culver produced a pen knife and carefully cut the little con's bonds. "I came out here, Bridwell, to hear you tell Pete Cordo what you wouldn't tell me. . . ."

Bridwell's face whitened. "I . . . Culver, I wasn't holding out. Honest to God. I did get those papers before the gang got there, but I was afraid to tell you. Doc Bromley up at the big house told me you were square and that you'd help me if I was. Honest, Culver, I was afraid you wouldn't believe me about the murder if I admitted about those papers."

Culver looked into the man's faded eyes and saw earnestness there. He waved indifferently. "Okay, Bridwell. It turned out for the best anyway. I did you a dirty trick and used you for bait to get Pete Cordo out some place where I could work on him."

Bridwell swallowed hard. "He . . . that, is he?"

Culver nodded. "Yes," he said curtly. "He is."

CHAPTER NINE

Who Killed O'Ryan?

IT WAS quiet in the big room at the old Cider Mill, doubly quiet in the memory of booming guns that had awakened echoes just a few short minutes before. Beau Bridwell cleared his throat.

"There's another feller in there, Culver. Feller that Cordo brought out here when he brought me."

Culver stiffened. He shook his head, then his jaw snapped. He had forgotten Dick Harper. With a muttered curse, he rose, entered the other room and cut the bonds from the securely tied and thoroughly scared mobster.

"You, Culver? What was. . . ."

"Never mind. You don't have to know."

Culver herded his man savagely into the other room. Harper stopped short and Bridwell came to his feet with a sharp gasp. Bridwell broke the silence first.

"Dick Harper. How in hell?"

Culver frowned. This wasn't in his scenario. "Do you know this mutt, Bridwell?"

The query was inane, but Culver's brain was numb. Bridwell nodded. "I sure do. Dick used to be a competitor of mine. You remember, Culver, I told you that there were only a few fellers could open a can by listening to the tumblers and . . .''

A great weight dropped off Culver. He felt as though a wet sponge had been wiped across his brain. His jaw set hard and his eyes bored into Dick Harper's blotched face. ''So that's the racket,'' he growled. ''I wondered why Vito had you hanging around. You're the busy little can opener who gets dope out of other people's safes for Bart Brunderson, eh?''

Dick Harper cowered. He put up one shaking hand as though to protest and stopped in mid motion to rub his chin. Culver's eyes were gleaming. He whipped around once more to Beau Bridwell. ''Look at him again, Bridwell. Look at him closely. Do you see anything else familiar about him besides the fact that you know him? Look, man!''

Beau Bridwell's lips trembled. ''Why yes, I. . . .''

Culver wheeled again. Harper seemed folding up in his tracks. Culver levelled a finger at him and his voice snapped like a whip lash. ''You murdered Judge O'Ryan, you dirty mugg!''

''No. I never. . . .''

''You lie. Spit it out quick.'' Culver had his automatic in his hands. Dick Harper trembled, then a crafty look came into his eyes.

''Yeah. I did it,'' he said. ''I socked him with a hunk of pipe. Vito didn't let me have no gun because he'd kept me off the liquor, and he give me a shot o' coke instead and he wouldn't let me have no gun, and me, I wouldn't go on any job without no weapon at all, and I dragged that hunk o' pipe.''

THE WORDS were tumbling out now as though the man had been longing to claim the most sensational murder of the decade. Culver stopped him with one savage gesture. ''What did you need a weapon for? Vito had a gun, didn't he? And Vito was along.''

Dick Harper stepped right into the trap. ''Sure. But that wasn't like me having a gun. Like I told you, Vito didn't let me have no gun. It was good I had that hunk o' pipe. Vito, he didn't have no guts when the old man come down. Me, I was the feller stood there and let him have it. . . .''

''That's swell.'' Culver's lips twisted savagely. ''You ought to get publicity on that, Dick. You must sit down and write it all out. NOW.''

The crafty smile came back to Dick Harper's lips. ''No, ain't dumb,'' he said. ''I don't mind telling you fellers because you can't tell the cops after all this shooting around here.''

Culver lighted a cigarette. ''Something in that, Dick. Especially when Pete Cordo and Hymie Katz and Bill Gregory are lying around dead.'' His eyes narrowed. ''But wouldn't it be terrible, Dick, if you got shot accidentally in the foot and left away out here with those corpses? Especially, Dick, if somebody tipped off some of Cordo's mob and sent them out here. . . .''

The pallor in Dick Harper's face gave testimony of the fact that he was able to imagine some of the things that would happen. Culver took a note book out of his pocket, tore out a half dozen sheets and flipped his fountain pen on the table beside them. ''Get busy, Dick, and write. Be sure and mention Vito, too.''

With a sob in his throat, Dick Harper wrote.

Three quarters of an hour later, Culver left Beau Bridwell in his own rooms on guard over a sullen prisoner who had been somewhat mollified by the gift of a quart of Scotch. Under the mattress in the same room, without Dick Harper being at all aware of it, there reposed the papers of Judge O'Ryan retrieved on the way from the tool shed behind his house.

''Bridwell,'' he said as he left, ''watch that mugg close. One hour before you're scheduled to do what I told you to do, you let him loose.''

''You mean free, altogether?'' Bridwell was incredulous.

''Yeah. That's it. Let him roam.''

With a casual wave, Dean Culver went down the hall. From a phone booth down stairs, he called the *Press Courier*. When he came out, he was smiling grimly. The Blue Barrel had the front page again, but the fun was just starting. He was levelling down the sights at last at the man he wanted to get.

CHAPTER TEN

THE PAY-OFF

A THOUSAND passers-by might walk the narrow street on which the two story headquarters of Bart Brunderson stood, without noticing anything about the building except that the windows were dirty and that it was difficult to read the sign which carried the legend ''Bartholomew Brunderson—Real Estate.'' To those in the know, the faded sign was no more important than the dirty windows. Bart Brunderson was in the real estate business only when the city was contemplating the purchase of land for some purpose. At such times, Black Bart always had advance information and options on the desired property snugly tucked away. His real estate profits on such deals were enormous, but they represented only a fraction of the business that he did in the shabby building.

It was dark outside when Dean Culver came to the building as a distant clock chimed the half hour after nine. There was light behind the dirty windows, however, and the sound of laughter came from within. Culver smiled and mounted the steps. He turned the knob of the front door and let himself into a semi-dark hallway. The voices in the big room off to the left hushed as his footsteps sounded. He turned toward the light and stepped into the room.

Black Bart was sitting with his face toward the door, but the eagerness of his expression faded into puzzled anger when he recognized the intruder. Vito Torino, whose chair had been tilted back against the wall, let his heels click on the floor. A dozen ward heelers, gangsters and hangers-on looked at Culver as a wolf pack might look at a prospective victim. Culver removed his hat and brushed some imaginary dust from about the bullet hole in the alpine.

''Good evening, gentlemen,'' he said softly, ''did I intrude on a meeting.''

Black Bart's eyes retreated behind the fatty pouches that hid them opportunely at times. He rolled a dead cigar the full length of his lips and back again. The mysterious taking off of Pete Cordo at about the hour that Culver had been scheduled to die was a blow to Bart Brunderson, and he had not yet figured it out. While the papers were busy laying the killing to a war with the Torino mob, Bart Brunderson knew differently. In a game where knowledge is power, he found himself suddenly without knowledge on a subject of importance. He had already played with the idea of making terms with Culver at almost any price. It wasn't a nice thought but it was preferable to the nasty question in Vito Torino's eyes. Culver's sudden appearance in this gathering called his hand. He had to be a friend or an enemy of Culver's and the mob was waiting for his decision. He shifted his body uncomfortably.

"How are you, Culver?" He compromised. "Want to sit around and wait for the cops?"

CULVER raised his eyes innocently, too innocently. "You haven't got anything to do with the cops, I hope?" His tone was mocking. Black Bart's eyes, hidden in the folds of fat, had been sizing up the room. The wolves were hostile to Culver, definitely hostile—and this time the lead wolf had to run with the pack. He couldn't risk a challenge of his leadership. Too many things had gone wrong lately. His lips curled.

"Culver," he growled. "You don't fool me a bit. I told you before and I'm telling you again that I hate your guts. You ain't regular. That crack I made about the cops was sarcasm, see? Scram. I figured you for a stool, see."

The pack was leaning forward now, applauding silently. Culver blew on his hat and quietly replaced it. He was looking calmly at Bart Brunderson but his attention was on the little office off in the corner; the office which opened on the areaway and that was separated from this room by a thin partition. That office wasn't important normally; it was a blind and a shabby pretense of a place where nothing important was kept. Tonight it was very important. Culver yawned.

"I'm disappointed, Brunderson," he said, "to find you in such bum humor. You were laughing when I came in. You wouldn't be worried about a sucker you framed off the press would you?"

He looked around the room as he spoke. Anything to keep their attention for a while. Brunderson paled. He was conscious of something under the surface and he was suddenly alarmed. He had been confidently waiting for his laugh on the District Attorney. Now some sense told him that Culver was connected with that joke of his somehow and that it might possibly turn out wrong. His coarse features worked.

"You're damned right," he snarled viciously. "I had you kicked off the sheets and I can brush you aside again if you get in my way; anything from picking pockets to murder—I'll hang it on you and make it stick. Now, get the hell out of here!"

He stood up as he spoke and there was a general tensing. Culver felt a tightening along his own spine. Time was his enemy and he had to whip Time into submission, stall, hold this crowd. He ignored the damning admission that had caused specks of red to dance before his eyes. He held his voice down, his features rigid.

"Would you like to know, Brunderson," he asked quietly, "just what happened to Pete Cordo and why?"

Black Bart's jaw dropped and a sibilant hiss ran around the room. Culver knew that he could commit suicide very easily in the next few minutes, but he remembered, too, that this crowd was waiting for a raid. They'd be careful here. Vito Torino was on his feet, his dark eyes flashing.

"What you know about the Cordo bump?" he challenged.

Culver shrugged. "I know you didn't do it, Vito," he said. "I got a tip that Pete was rubbed out because he was after the O'Ryan papers. I don't know."

THERE WAS no need for artificial means of holding this crowd's attention now. They would not have heard a trap drum in the little room beyond the partition. Black Bart was gripping the back of his chair.

"Who—who did it?" he gasped.

Culver made a gesture of bewilderment. "I don't know," he said, "but I got a phone call . . ."

He stopped there. Someone was whistling "After the Ball Was Over" out on the street. It was his signal. Culver relaxed and lighted a cigarette. His job was done. The crowd was shooting questions in machine gun fashion. Culver raised his hands.

"Hell, I can't answer all those. I thought Brunderson might know who wanted those papers and that he'd be able to tell who killed Pete Cordo."

"But why did anyone call you?" A ward boss threw the question from the corner of the room. Culver looked grave.

"There was a rumor out that Pete was going to have me bumped. This guy on the phone was friendly. He thought if I knew that Pete was going after those papers that I'd maybe rig a deal to work with him."

A whistle shrilled out in the street. Culver sat back in his chair and every eye turned to the door. Black Bart, master of himself for the moment, rose to his feet. A tramp of feet sounded in the hall and the frail figure of J. Gordon Joyce stood framed in the doorway. With a dramatic gesture, the District Attorney waved a paper.

"Brunderson," he shrilled, "I have a warrant to search . . ."

Black Bart laughed. "Search away, my hearty. Good luck to you."

Pale, uncertain and patently shaking, J. Gordon Joyce waved the police to their task. He had been talked into making this raid and he was trembling inside. They made quick work of the room in which the meeting was held and moved on the private office. Brunderson crowded in with them. Culver stood in the doorway. He could feel the pressure of the crowd at his back and he politely made room for Vito Torino, ushering him well up front.

Half-heartedly, the police started to turn out drawers while Bart Brunderson stood with his thumbs hooked in his suspenders and kidded them. "If you'll tell me what you're looking for, I'll help," he jeered.

J. Gordon Joyce crossed to the safe and gave the dial a turn. He had been told to do that, too, and he did it without confidence. The door opened and Bart Brunderson's jests died on his lips. He stiffened. The District Attorney reached inside the safe and pulled out a thick sheaf of papers. He gave a grunt of satisfaction. His eyes raised accusingly to Black Bart.

"These papers, Mr. Brunderson," he said coldly, "are the private papers of Judge O'Ryan; the evidence which he collected to show that you—and not Governor Barker—were the inspiration of graft and corruption in this city."

THE CROWD behind Culver was moving restlessly and Culver could almost hear the thought-wheels whir. He had planted an idea and these men were sure now that Torino's gang had killed Cordo for these very papers. If they hadn't why hadn't Brunderson admitted having them?

Black Bart was white and he was leaning heavily against the wall. "I've been framed," he yelled. "It's a dirty frame. It won't hold up in court . . ."

"Oh, yes, it will." The District Attorney's voice was cold steel. "Do you think that you—with your reputation — can convict me of crooked methods. This, Man, is evidence."

He drew a sharp breath and literally hurled his next verbal bombshell. "Moreover," he said, "we have the murderer of Judge O'Ryan, self-confessed, at headquarters with a full confession of his accomplice and . . . Stop him!"

Vito Torino turned to flee and a heavy handed cop caught him and swung him around. He snarled at Black Bart. "Wise guy," he shouted. "Wise guy, ain't you . . ."

The rest was silenced as he was bundled out of the room. Black Bart rode with him in the hurry wagon.

Out on the sidewalk before the grimy building that had been the Brunderson nest of corruption for so long, Dean Culver stood with his hands in his pockets. "Pete Cordo died with a gun in his fist," he murmured, "and Black Bart hollers 'frame.' Some smart egg wrote once that 'they die by the sword who live by the sword' and ain't it the truth? Maybe it was dirty to have Beau Bridwell tap that can and plant the evidence, but how can you get rid of a dirty framer unless you frame him? The answer is that you can't."

The crowd had scattered to spread the word through the underworld where each man would interpret the facts according to his lights. Some would read into Brunderson's possession of the papers a link with the killing of Pete Cordo; other, more thoughtful souls, would smell a frame-up and pay off silently on a new force in the field of crime, an unseen worker behind the scenes who had been big enough to make a sucker out of Black Bart.

Dean Culver turned back to the deserted office. Over Bart Brunderson's own phone, he called Joe Loftus, City Editor of the *Press Courier*. Culver had spent four and a half hours when he was loggy for sleep in copying the important papers of the O'Ryan collection. Those papers, with a pre-written story had gone to Loftus by special messenger just before Culver entered Brunderson's.

"Blue Barrel," he snapped. "The story goes as you've got it. Everything clicked like a puzzle.

Perfect. Shoot it and—wait a minute!" A smile creased his hard features. "Bart Brunderson offered five grand for the killers of the Judge," he said slowly. It was just a gesture, but he ought to pay for bum gestures. Collect it for me."

HE TURNED from the phone. Outside there was an off-key whistler rendering the dolorous strains of "After the Ball Was Over." Culver went out to meet Beau Bridwell and, for the first time, he shook hands with him.

"You're clear, Old Timer," he said, "and the governor's clear and the only people who are hurt are people who had it coming." His eyes warmed. "You did one whale of a fast job on that safe. Great. I'm going to see that you get a stake."

Bridwell stammered, his pale eyes glowing. "Aw, that can was pie," he said. "Kids in short pants was opening that kind when I was in my prime. . . ."

Culver was frowning with a sudden recollection. "Tell me something," he said. "Why in blazes did you climb out an upstairs window at O'Ryan's when it was easier to get out downstairs. I can't figure that play if you did it."

The look of awe which was habitually on Beau Bridwell's face when he looked at Dean Culver faded. His chest swelled with the pride of a vindicated old timer who knows his ropes.

"Anybody ought to figure that," he said condescendingly. "Those other guys came in after me, didn't they? They used my entry, didn't they? Hell's Bells! Was I going to walk out into the arms of their lookout?"

A sheepish smile crossed Culver's face. "And I was just thinking that I was smart," he said. "Well that just goes to show something or another. Shut up about it, Bridwell, and I'll buy you a drink."

Together they went to Big John Zoro's.

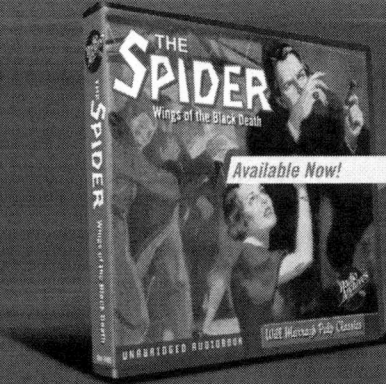

Printed in Great Britain
by Amazon